This Storied River

This Storied River

～

**Legend & Lore
of the Upper Mississippi**

Dennis McCann

WISCONSIN HISTORICAL SOCIETY PRESS

Published by the Wisconsin Historical Society Press
Publishers since 1855

The Wisconsin Historical Society helps people connect to the past by collecting, preserving, and sharing stories. Founded in 1846, the Society is one of the nation's finest historical institutions.

Order books by phone toll free: (888) 999-1669
Order books online: shop.wisconsinhistory.org
Join the Wisconsin Historical Society: wisconsinhistory.org/membership

Photographs identified with WHI or WHS are from the Society's collections; address requests to reproduce these photos to the Visual Materials Archivist at the Wisconsin Historical Society, 816 State Street, Madison, WI 53706.

All maps by Mapping Specialists, Ltd., Fitchburg, WI

Printed in the United States of America
Cover design by Diana Boger
Interior typesetting by Biner Design

21 20 19 18 17   1 2 3 4 5
Library of Congress Cataloging-in-Publication Data
Names: McCann, Dennis, 1950– author.
Title: This storied river : legend and lore of the upper Mississippi /
    Dennis McCann.
Description: Madison, WI : Wisconsin Historical Society Press, 2017. |
    Includes bibliographical references and index.
Identifiers: LCCN 2016045190 (print) | LCCN 2016046086 (e-book) | ISBN
    9780870207846 (paperback : alkaline paper) | ISBN 9780870207853 (e-book) |
Subjects: LCSH: Mississippi River Region—History, Local—Anecdotes. |
    Wisconsin—History, Local—Anecdotes. | Middle West—History,
    Local—Anecdotes. | Mississippi River Region—Biography—Anecdotes. |
    Mississippi River Region—Social life and customs—Anecdotes. |
    Folklore—Mississippi River Region.
Classification: LCC F351 .M123 2017 (print) | LCC F351 (e-book) | DDC
    398.20977—dc23
LC record available at https://lccn.loc.gov/2016045190

♾ The paper used in this publication meets the minimum requirements of the American National Standard for Information Sciences—Permanence of Paper for Printed Library Materials, ANSI Z39.48–1992.

For Barbara, of course.
We'll always have Lake Pepin.

WHI IMAGE ID 75474

Contents

1

Up the Famous River, Again

In 1854 the Chicago & Rock Island Railroad sponsored the grandest excursion the young United States had ever experienced.

It was called, naturally, the Grand Excursion. More than a thousand participants—investors, bankers, politicians, scholars, journalists, and even a few regular people—boarded trains in Chicago and at other stops en route and were carried to Rock Island, across the Mississippi River from Davenport, Iowa, where they boarded a flotilla of steamboats and headed north on a journey of discovery.

The Grand Excursion was an opportunity for the Chicago & Rock Island Railroad to celebrate its status as the first railroad company to reach the Mississippi and, its sights already on expansion even farther west, to introduce influential Americans to the verdant river valley and the immense opportunity it presented.

It was not the first exploration of the Mississippi; smaller parties, from traders to trappers and more, had been using the river as transport for hundreds of years, and the steamship *Virginia* had carried the first small retinue of passengers upriver in 1823. Nor was the landscape the excursionists witnessed classic wilderness.

A sternwheel excursion on the Mississippi River. WHI IMAGE ID 6074

It was, of course, a land of soaring bluffs, wooded isles, free-flowing main channels, and sprawling sloughs that satisfied romantic dreams of the wild frontier. Already, though, a few small, rough settlements dotted the river's banks, and more would-be residents had been drifting in to a countryside long populated by Indians.

But in scope and scale, the Grand Excursion went above and beyond all previous explorations. The *New York Tribune* called it "one of the grandest entertainments imagined," while the *Chicago Tribune* settled on "the most brilliant party ever assembled in the west." One writer on the trip called the scenery "over 150 miles of unimaginable fairyland, genie-land and world of vision," while the *New Haven Register* described the traveling party as "the largest, longest and most respectable ever 'got up' since the days of Moses and the Children of Israel." Perhaps the most distinguished

excursionist, former US president Millard Fillmore, said of his experience, "There will never be another such excursion, nor another such jubilee."

Yet there would be. In 2004, on the 150th anniversary of the Grand Excursion, communities both large and small from the four states along the Upper Mississippi re-created the original expedition, rounding up enough paddleboats to carry hundreds of modern-day excursionists along the same route.

Millard Fillmore couldn't make this trip, but I did.

How could I not? At the time I was a traveling columnist for the *Milwaukee Journal Sentinel*, and the chance to follow in the wandering steps of Moses and the Children of Israel—never mind their river was the Nile and not the Mississippi—was too tempting to resist. The grandest entertainment imagined? I could only imagine, but I persuaded my editor that if I took part, I could know for sure. So, when the participants of Grand Excursion 2.0 assembled in the Quad Cities that summer and boarded boats for a five-day slow float upriver, I boarded with them.

Despite ten years of planning the sesquicentennial trip, there was one hitch no one could do anything to prevent. Thanks to heavy rains in the weeks before the trip was scheduled to begin, the river was high and rising—so high that the two biggest stars of the flotilla, the elegant paddleboats *Delta Queen* and *Mississippi Queen*, were caught up in Hannibal, Missouri, unable to slide under the railroad bridge until the water subsided.

"You know what," excursion chairman Chris Mason told participants on the eve of our departure, "the mighty Mississippi is still mighty, and she's showing her might."

But smaller boats were on hand. The *Harriet Bishop*, the *Spirit of Peoria*, the *Anson Northrup*, and two others were ready and waiting when the mayor of Davenport, Iowa, Charlie Brook, sliced a welcome banner with a long sword and declared the excursion a go. We may not have shouted "Ho, for the Falls of St. Anthony!" as the early excursionists had, but the spirit was there as we set off for a long, languid ride on the most captivating waterway in America.

Up through Iowa and Illinois we went, then into Wisconsin and Minnesota. Many communities along the route used the occasion to show off recent civic improvements or to launch new ones inspired by the extra attention being paid the river. It was not entirely incident-free—in Clayton, Iowa, volunteer firefighters came with a tanker truck when the *Anson Northrup* found itself without water—but the excursion was a big deal on water and on land. For those not aboard riverboats, there were concerts and reenactments, painters and film festivals. Many gathered at the river's edge to watch us pass, envy on their faces. On the boats we were treated to educational lectures, lots of quiet time to gaze at the stunning river and the majestic bluffs and quiet little river

Passengers disembark a Mississippi River boat, while a large crowd gathers on the shore. WHI IMAGE ID 71939

towns along its shores, and, for some, perhaps a bit more banjo playing than the recommended daily allowance.

"If you are the sort of person who enjoys quiet music early in the morning," I wrote in one story, "imagine a three-banjo band strumming 'Up the Lazy River' an hour before breakfast and you'll never take Mozart for granted again."

Did my descriptions match the breathless encomiums written by my predecessor scribes? Was it the grandest entertainment I could have imagined? That's difficult to measure, because I'd had lots of great experiences as a traveling columnist with a decent expense account. But one memory stands out, the evening when the golden light of day's end flooded over our flotilla, joined at this point by the elegant *Delta Queen*, as we neared Prairie du Chien, "the *Delta's* big wheel turning, the *Julia Belle Swain's* calliope filling the summer night with song and the *Northrup* just behind, freshly watered. Over Prairie du Chien, hot air balloons rose and disappeared over the trees," I wrote. "It was a Tina Turner moment on America's River."

(There was also a moment of ick. After thousands of people cheered our arrival in Dubuque, millions of mayflies hatched overnight and sent us off the next morning. As I told our readers, "They darkened the walls of our hotel, slicked the sidewalks with their slimy corpses, lit on hats and shirts and fell down necks. It was a biblical plague, Iowa-style."

Once again, the river was just being the river. Mayflies— technically not flies at all, but members of the order *Ephemeroptera*—spend most of their yearlong lifespan underwater, emerging only to mate and die. Hatches are big, messy, and sometimes dangerous. In 2012 a hatch left a four-inch layer of mayfies on Highway 61 near Hastings, so slick that a driver lost control and hit another vehicle. In 2014 the hatch was so large that weather radar registered it as a rainfall; for the heaviest hatches, snowplows are brought out of summer hibernation.

Still, mayflies are considered a good thing because they're a sign of healthy water. The 2004 excursion was not only a re-creation of the original exploration but also a celebration of the health of the river.)

America's River. The Mighty Mississippi. Old Man River and Big Muddy. The Mississippi River has more aliases than any post office wall, and every one is an apt description of the waterway that both divides these United States and unites them. It is, as the historians Stephen E. Ambrose and Douglas Brinkley wrote in *The Mississippi and the Making of a Nation*, 2,350 miles of America's lifeblood—"the vital economic engine and the mythic symbol that flows through our history, our continent, our music, our literature, our lives."

Or, as Garrison Keillor says in the video that greets visitors to the very fine National Mississippi River Museum in Dubuque, "It comes at us bigger than life. The Mississippi—artery of a continent, lifeblood of a country."

It is the river of Mark Twain and the watery setting for *The Adventures of Huckleberry Finn*, which more than a few readers and critics think is the finest single piece of literature our country has produced. It is the river of Mike Fink, the "king of the keel boaters," whose legends on the river rival those of Paul Bunyan in the woods. It is the river of Native Americans for whom it was both highway and homeland long before it was "discovered" by the first white men. And for the voyageurs Marquette and Joliet, for the steamboat pilots, settlers, shippers, clammers, pearlers, fishermen, paddlers, and the legion of waterside residents who proudly call themselves river rats, the Mississippi is home, come hell or high water—and all too often, one of those does.

"It doesn't matter from what perspective you look at the river in the middle of the continent—geologically, ecologically, prehistorically, ethnographically, economically, industrially, socially, musically, literarily, culturally, or over the gunnels of your canoe midstream," wrote Paul Schneider in *Old Man River: The Mississippi River in North American History*. "It's hard to imagine America without the Mississippi. The river's history is our history."

Yet today's river is not the same water paddled by Marquette and Joliet, described by Twain, or taken on by steamboat pilots. Once, the river truly had a mind of its own, able to shift course so abruptly that a farm built on one bank might suddenly find itself on the other. It had hundreds of tributaries, many hundreds more islands, countless snags and eddies and an often-unruly disposition that bested many who took it on.

An iconic view of Mississippi River life by famed river photographer Gerhard Gesell. WHI IMAGE ID 3549

Then white people came along in large numbers and with them came a need to move ever greater quantities of goods, people, animals, and more not only *down* the Mississippi, which was its natural course, but also upriver against the current, a far trickier proposition. Snags were cleared and wing dams built to better direct the current. Most dramatically, the need for a nine-foot-deep channel for shipping ever bigger boats and barges led to a series of locks and dams that turned a free-flowing river of more than 2,300 miles into a series of more than two dozen pools—a stairway of river, in effect.

The Mississippi "is now for all intents and purposes a man-made artifact," Lee Sandlin contends in *Wicked River: The Mississippi When It Last Ran Wild*. "The Mississippi has been dredged, and walled in, and reshaped, and fixed; it has been turned into a gigantic navigation canal, or the world's largest industrial sewer. It hasn't run wild as a river does in nature for more than a hundred years."

Yet the Mississippi runs wild in our imaginations. While much of its shore is lined by cities large and small, by bluff-top human aeries with million-dollar views, and by farms, railroad tracks,

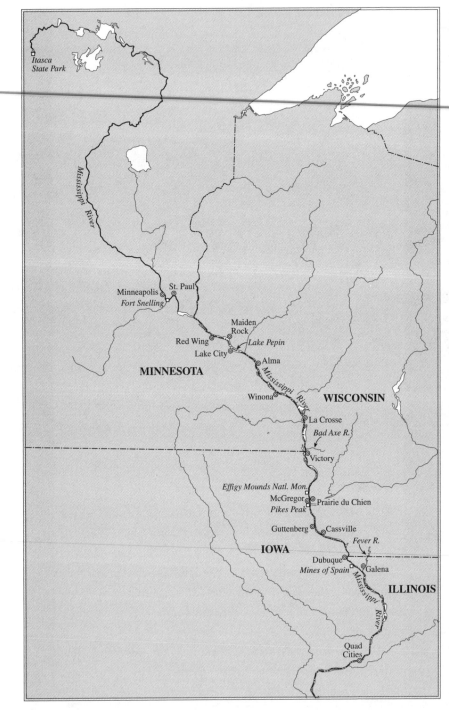

The Upper Mississippi River.

grain silos and more, large stretches are still at least wild looking, with great stone bluffs and deep green forests. And it is still home to a huge population of wild things—the National Park Service says at least 260 species of fish swim its waters, 40 percent of our migratory birds use its corridor for spring and fall migration, and 60 percent of all birds use the Mississippi River Basin as their migratory flyway.

For millions of Americans it is a flyway of sorts, as well. The Great River Road National Scenic Byway tracks the journey of the river for more than three thousand miles, from northern Minnesota to the Gulf of Mexico, a route identified by the familiar green pilot's wheel logo. The designation recognizes "the river's outstanding assets in the areas of culture, history, nature, recreation, and scenic beauty."

The route can be driven in as little as thirty-six hours, but only a fool or fleeing felon would choose that. Far better to take days, to cross from side to side, climb overlooks to look over, and try to never pass by a historical marker without stopping to read.

In their book, written on the two hundredth anniversary of the Louisiana Purchase that added the Mississippi River to American holdings, Ambrose and Brinkley "decided early on we couldn't possibly write a history of the river—that would mean volumes."

I wholeheartedly agree. And so, echoing the Grand Excursion writer who warned his readers to "believe no man, but see for yourselves the Mississippi River above Dubuque," this is a book about just one part of the Mississippi, the upper stretch beginning at, yes, Dubuque. It is not a guidebook, though places of historical interest come with each chapter. It is meant more as a historical primer on just a few of the countless stories to which the river has given life over the past two centuries.

The stories in this collection were not those I wrote on the occasion of that 2004 expedition. Instead, they come from my longtime exploration of the Upper Mississippi as a traveling newspaperman, from reading extensively about the river from those who know it well, and from research at museums and historic sites specifically for this book. Stories are arranged roughly in order from south to north, which is the same direction taken by early explorers searching for the Mississippi's elusive headwaters. I could have set them from north to south, which is as the river flows, but there's one other reason for beginning where we do. The National Mississippi River Museum, in Dubuque, is the perfect place to start your own Grand Excursion of this storied river.

2

Julien Dubuque and the Mines of Spain

For more than a century, the Julien Dubuque monument, a castlelike limestone tower that overlooks Catfish Creek in the Mines of Spain Recreation Area just south of Dubuque, has served to honor and remember the city's founder. More than that, Dubuque was also a fur trader, lead

miner, entrepreneur, hail fellow well met, and namesake for the historic city on the Mississippi River.

In today's terms Dubuque might have been something of a confidence man, given his ability to so thoroughly ingratiate himself with Indians in the lead region that they freely gave him rights to mine iron ore on their lands, which he then contrived to claim for his own. Still, such was Dubuque's attachment to the Meskwaki people that upon his death, the Indian people among whom he had worked and lived competed for the honor of carrying his casket to his burial site on the bluff at Catfish Creek. There, Dubuque's grave was marked by a wooden cross and the epitaph "Mineur des Mines d'Espagne"—Miner of the Mines of Spain.

A French Canadian, Julien Dubuque was born in 1762 on the banks of the St. Lawrence River near Quebec. He was educated in both French and English, developed an appreciation for the arts as well as music, and became an adept fiddler as a young man. He worked as a clerk out of Michilimackinac, on modern-day Mackinac Island, where he learned about trading with Indians, until reports of rich lead deposits prompted him to join his brother at Prairie du Chien around 1783. Traveling downriver, Dubuque settled among the Meskwaki, who were engaged in mining iron ore, and he soon earned their respect and friendship. By 1788, Dubuque made an agreement with the Meskwaki led by Aquoqua, or Kettle Chief, giving him sole permission to work the lead mines near Catfish Creek.

Thomas Auge, a longtime history professor who wrote extensively about Dubuque's early days, noted in the Iowa Historical Society's *The Palimpsest* that such permission was "a remarkable and valuable concession, a triumph for Dubuque, one which virtually assured him an important role in the culture of the Upper Mississippi. The lead region which the Meskwakis controlled had long been considered a prize of great wealth."

Dubuque was a relative newcomer with no experience in mining, and historians don't know exactly how he was granted such a great favor. Some believe it was because he married into the tribe, though other French traders did so without being granted such rights.

The more often-told legend is more fun, if not reliably based.

"A popular explanation for the grant by the Indians is that he had convinced them he possessed magical supernatural powers," Auge wrote. "One story relates that he could handle rattlesnakes without harm. Another tells how he threatened to burn the river if the Indians did not give him what he wanted. He allegedly had oil secretly poured on the water which burst into flames when he fired it, to the astonishment and fear of the Indians.

"These accounts of duping the Indians into believing that he possessed magical powers are, however, only legends and do not rest upon reliable eyewitness accounts. Still, the existence of such legends does indicate that Dubuque's position with the Indians was extraordinary."

However tenuous his claim, Dubuque went to work, building cabins for his French Canadian workers, a smelting furnace, trading post, sawmill, and other structures. The agreement with the Meskwaki stipulated that he could mine the land as long as he wished, but Dubuque went beyond even that, claiming that the deal gave him actual possession of the land and asking the Spanish governor of Louisiana to recognize his right.

By Auge's account, Dubuque was seeking land far greater than that he had been given permission to mine, which he could then sell or deed to others.

"Clearly, Julien Dubuque was engaging in a common frontier practice: cheating the Indians of their lands," Auge wrote.

Mines of Spain Recreation Area, present-day. RONALD W. TIGGES, DIGITALDUBUQUE.COM

"Considering the Indians' kindness toward Dubuque, as well as the years he spent living and working with them, his scheme ~~has an aura of duplicity unusual even in dealings with the Indians.~~" Eventually the Spanish government granted him a tract of land stretching twenty-one miles long and nine miles wide—thus, the Mines of Spain. While the US government later approved his claim, it was contested after his death in litigation that lingered for more than forty years before the US Supreme Court finally invalidated it in 1854.

At their peak, the mines were productive and profitable enough to reward Dubuque with a lavish lifestyle and burden him with debts as a result. He shipped hundreds of thousands of pounds of lead while also staying involved with the fur trade, but his financial woes were such that he was forced to sell half of his land to a partner and he died, at age forty-eight, still in debt.

There was no mention of a wife in his will but there are historical references to Dubuque having been married to Potosa, daughter of his friend, the Meskwaki chief Peosta, who was later buried on the bluff with Dubuque.

A little wooden hut was placed over Dubuque's grave in the Meskwaki tradition, but over time it deteriorated, and souvenir hunters stole the cross. By the end of the nineteenth century some with an eye toward history called for a marker suitable for the city's namesake. One J. H. Stevenson even put his request in verse:

A few short years, and who can tell
That here his grave was ever made
Since neither slab nor shaft appears
To indicate where he was laid.
O people of Dubuque, for shame!
No longer suffer such disgrace;
But raise a shaft above his tomb,
To mark his final resting place.

Julien Dubuque Monument. RONALD W. TIGGES, DIGITALDUBUQUE.COM

In 1895, a committee of the Dubuque Old Settlers Association took on the task. When the site was excavated, several skeletons were found, including Dubuque's and one believed to be that of Peosta. But when the stone monument was finished a few years later, only Dubuque was reburied there. Peosta's skeleton was left in a local museum until the 1960s, when the treatment of Native American remains became a sensitive issue. In 1973, with the consent and cooperation of tribal leaders, Peosta's remains were reburied with Dubuque on the bluff, where the chairman of the Meskwaki Indian Settlement at Tama, Iowa, said, "The friendship shows us the way toward having the type of society we should have—a society existing in friendship and peace."

Julien Dubuque's name held a prominent place in the city of Dubuque. In 1854 the former Waples Hotel was renamed Hotel Julien. After that structure burned in 1913 a new Hotel Julien opened, which was rechristened the Hotel Julien Dubuque after extensive renovation in 2009. Among its themed specialty suites is one named for the gangster Al Capone, who was said to have often hidden out in Dubuque when Chicago got too hot.

One other notable, if odiferous, historical event took place at the Hotel Julien in 1935. A doctor in Independence, Iowa, prescribed Limburger cheese, made in Monroe, Wisconsin, for a patient with digestive problems; but after a mail carrier complained of the odor, the local postmaster banned its delivery. He sent it back to Monroe with the explanation that it could "fell an ox at 20 paces." This so incensed the Monroe postmaster that he challenged his Iowa counterpart to a "sniffing duel" at the Hotel Julien in Dubuque.

Newspapers across the country hyped the duel ("Limburger: Fragrant in Monroe, Putrid in Iowa" was the *Milwaukee Journal*'s headline, while famed writer Richard S. Davis called it "a duel to the breath"), and a large contingent of reporters attended the showdown. But when Monroe postmaster John Burkhard, after praising the cheese's medicinal qualities, passed a chunk of smelly cheese, a clothespin, and a gas mask to Independence postmaster Warren Miller, he put up his hands and surrendered. "I won't need the clothespin," he said. "I haven't any sense of smell."

PLACES OF INTEREST

Mines of Spain Recreation Area/E. B. Lyons Interpretive Center, 8991 Bellevue Heights, Dubuque. The site includes hiking trails, the Julien Dubuque monument, and scenic views. www.minesofspain.org

Hotel Julien Dubuque, 200 Main Street, www.hotel juliendubuque.com

Mathias Ham House Museum, 2241 Lincoln Avenue, shares stories of early Dubuque and Victorian life. www.rivermuseum.com/exhibits-experiences/ mathias-ham-house

National Mississippi River Museum & Aquarium, 350 E. 3rd St., www.rivermusuem.com

3

Boom Town on the Fever

On one of a number of occasions
when newspaper business brought
me to Galena, I checked into the
DeSoto House Hotel, making sure
to request a second-floor room over-
looking downtown's Main Street.
Unfortunately, today's guests are
not able to step out onto the narrow

balcony that lines the front of the hotel, but I could imagine what
it might be like to stand on that historic structure, an audience
of thousands on the streets below, hanging on your every word.

Even in one of the most historic and scrupulously preserved
cities along the Mississippi River—fully 85 percent of Galena is
listed on the National Register of Historic Places—the DeSoto
House Hotel and its balcony stand out for their roles in the past.

On July 23, 1856, one year after the then five-story hotel had
been built and billed as "the largest and most luxurious hotel in
the West," Abraham Lincoln stepped onto the balcony to speak
on behalf of Republican presidential candidate John Freemont. A
large crowd gathered to hear Lincoln's message of national unity,
which included the line "We WON'T dissolve the Union, and
you SHAN'T!"

Two years later, Lincoln's rival Stephen Douglas spoke from the same balcony. Thousands rallied there on Lincoln's behalf in 1860. When the Civil War ended and former Galena resident Ulysses S. Grant returned in triumph on August 16, 1865, a huge arch across Main Street at the hotel read, "Hail to the Chief Who in Triumph Advances." A crowd said to number twenty-five thousand was on hand to do just that. And in 1868 candidate Grant made rooms 209 and 211 of the hotel his campaign headquarters while running for president.

The earliest-known portrait of Abraham Lincoln, created just a few years before his speech at the DeSoto House Hotel. WHI IMAGE ID 23606

The DeSoto House does not look today precisely as it did in Lincoln and Grant's day—the top two stories were removed for safety reasons in 1880—but if its oft-renovated remaining walls could tell stories, they would tell wondrous tales about a river town and its glory days.

As it happens, Galena is not on the Mississippi but five miles away on the Galena River, a tributary that in the city's early days was called the Fever River—and more's the pity (though perhaps not for modern tourism boosters) that colorful name was forever erased. Still, in its heyday Galena was a busy and important port for Mississippi River steamboats carrying away the underground treasures of the region. The treasure was lead, which caused a rush in Galena—the Latin word for lead sulfide—decades before gold did the same in California.

Native Americans had long mined lead for tools and weapons before Frenchman Nicolas Perrot arrived in 1690 to build a trading post on the east side of the Mississippi across from present-day Dubuque. But the real boom began in the early 1800s. In 1816 Colonel George Davenport, after whom Davenport, Iowa, would be named, shipped the first boatload of lead ore down the Fever to the Mississippi and beyond. Two years later the first cabin was built on the Fever, and soon one hundred men from St. Louis came upriver to mine for lead.

Four years later, large groups of miners from Kentucky arrived, and as steamboat traffic increased, miners from Tennessee, Virginia, southern Illinois, and other places arrived to work the lead leases in northern Illinois and southwestern Wisconsin. (Those southern roots would lead to mixed sympathies in the region where the northern cause's future hero resided as the Civil War approached.) The rush grew more intense in the years after the Black Hawk War, which ended fears of Indian hostilities. As Indian communities were left dispirited and often displaced to sites further west, white settlers arrived in ever greater numbers, and by 1845 lead ore production peaked at 54 million tons, or more than 80 percent of the national total.

"Galena in the boom years was a busy, boisterous town jammed between rocky hills, with houses which an eastern visitor compared to a flock of sheep going down to water," Walter Havighurst wrote in his book *Upper Mississippi: A Wilderness Saga.*

"Nearly every person in town could stand on his own front step and look down on the river where the steamboats churned in to the landing. When the long lines of ore wagons creaked through the streets and the steamers daily disgorged hundreds of new families eager to stake their claims in the district, Galena was vibrant with frontier energy and expectation. Thousands of people coming up the Fever River found a spirit unlike that of older regions of America. Here was the free, unbounded country, the new land teeming with life and bright with promise.

"There was, after all, a fever in that valley."

Almost all of the lead that spurred the fever was shipped out
of Galena on steamboats, which also brought curious "excursionists" to visit the bustling lead region. Galena grew quickly through
those years to a peak population of some fourteen thousand residents, and hundreds of handsome Victorian business structures,
residences for regular folks, and mansions for steamboat captains
and mine owners were built. So many survive today as to give
the city an appearance much like it wore 150 years ago. Some
have called Galena the "outdoor museum of the Victorian West."
General Grant, if he could return today, would feel right at home.

If it was lead that drove the economic engine, it was Grant
who put Galena on the map. He moved with his wife, Julia, and
four children to Galena in 1860, not to work the lead mines but to
labor, rather ignominiously, as clerk in his father's leather-goods
store, having done poorly at earlier business ventures. When the
Civil War began he was commissioned a colonel in the Illinois
militia and, of course, went on in 1864 to become general in chief
of all US forces.

Oddly, though, he was not the only resident of Galena to become a general in that conflict. It is with good reason that diners
at the DeSoto House gather in the Generals' Restaurant, because
nine Galenans would become generals by war's end, including

The DeSoto
House Hotel,
present-day.
COURTESY OF
THE DESOTO
HOUSE HOTEL

Ely Parker, a Seneca Indian originally from New York. Parker had come to the lead region to oversee construction of a customs house, built to register Upper Mississippi River steamboat cargoes, which would also serve as post office. There, Parker met Grant and later became a part of Grant's personal staff. The Customs House today is the second-longest continually operating post office in the country and the first to be named a "Great American Post Office" by the Smithsonian.

Before the war the Grants lived in a modest brick house they rented for about $100 a year. But after his triumphant return, a group of supportive Republicans presented his family with a stately brick home of Italianate style, a big step up from just a few years earlier.

Grant wasn't there for long, moving instead to Washington to work in war recovery efforts, but he continued to visit Galena even after his election as president. The home remained in his family's ownership, maintained by caretakers in the event he would need to spend time there again. On his last visits to Galena in 1880, according to an account at the Grant home, he found "a new sidewalk laid in front of the premises, the outbuildings repaired, the trees handsomely trimmed, a new and commodious washhouse built and other improvements made."

Aware of public interest in the home, the Grant children gave it to the city of Galena in 1904, with the understanding that it be kept as a memorial to the general. And visitors were appreciative, especially after road improvements early in the 1900s allowed them to come by car in such numbers as to create the city's first traffic jam in October 1927. "There were 1,300 visitors registered at the Grant Memorial Home," the *Galena Gazette* reported. "Autos blocked Bouthillier Street for an hour at a time."

The city, confronted with the heavy cost of maintaining the home, in 1931 deeded it to the State of Illinois, which today operates it as a Galena State Historic Site. Other official historic sites in the city are Old Market House, the commercial heart of Galena in the boom years, and Washburne House, where Grant waited for election returns with his friend, the influential Congressman Elihu Washburne.

However, the long shadow of a hometown president could not save Galena's main lifeblood. As demand for lead sharply fell, the city's population rapidly declined from its peak to about 3,400 early in the twenty-first century. For some years the city's economy languished, but Galena's historic architecture was eventually discovered by artists and related businesses, and now each year visitors flock to Galena as miners once did, though in far larger numbers and with more money to spend. Steamboats no longer ply the Galena River, so heavily silted over the years they could not if they wanted to, but on busy weekends in summer and fall Galena is again a boomtown.

PLACES OF INTEREST

Galena–Jo Daviess County Historical Society and U.S. Grant Museum, 211 S. Bench Street, Galena, www.galenahistory.org/

DeSoto House Hotel, 230 S. Main Street, http://desotohouse.com/

Ulysses S. Grant Home, 500 Bouthillier Street, open Wednesday–Sunday, www.granthome.com/index.htm

Old Market House, 123 N. Commerce Street, open daily, www.granthome.com/index.htm

Washburne House, 908 Third Street, open Fridays from May-October, http://www.granthome.com/index.htm

4

Stonefield on the River

About thirty miles south of Prairie
du Chien in Cassville, Wisconsin,
visitors will find Stonefield, a re-
created rural village and museum
that reflects farm life in the 1800s
and is perhaps best known for the
mansion home of Wisconsin's first
governor, Nelson Dewey.

Cassville, as it happens, was named for a governor, but it
wasn't Dewey, and if the dreams of its early founders had come
true, Wisconsin's capitol might today stand on the banks of the
Mississippi instead of on a leafy Madison square. Cassville was
named for Lewis Cass, the onetime governor of the Michigan
Territory. In the 1830s speculators who wanted the new territorial
capital placed there bought land and began work on a four-story
brick building, the Denniston Hotel, to house the new government. When Madison was selected instead, Cassville's bright
future dimmed considerably.

However, young Nelson Dewey, who had moved there to work
as a clerk for the unsuccessful land speculators Daniels, Denniston & Co., remained in the area. Dewey studied law, passed the
territorial bar exam, and began a law practice in nearby Lancaster.

The Denniston Hotel, after the fourth floor was removed in the 1940s.
WHI IMAGE ID 29799

He also did well with investments in land and lead mining and became involved in local and territorial government.

Oddly, the man who would become Wisconsin's first governor was not a stereotypical politician, at least in the glad-handing sense, but more an efficient administrator. Nonetheless, at the first state Democratic convention in 1848, sentiment was divided between factions from eastern and southwestern Wisconsin, and Dewey, who was not aligned with either side, was chosen as a compromise candidate for governor. He won the election and served two terms focused on establishing the new state government.

After his second term Dewey and his wife, Catherine, went back to Cassville and returned to private life. As the speculators had earlier, Dewey wanted great things for the community. He bought up land and began finishing the Denniston Hotel. By the 1860s Dewey's sprawling estate covered some two thousand acres along the Mississippi River north of Cassville and most

Stonefield. WHI IMAGE ID 102772

prominently featured the mansion he called "Stonefield," a three-story red brick home with elegant furnishings and stone barns and fences.

When times were good, Dewey was benevolent, employing anyone who needed work, even if not all the work really needed doing. Sometimes his workers built stone fences, not so much to enclose space or keep others out but mostly to give the men jobs.

But the lord of the manor's grasp on good times would not last. His relationship with Catherine suffered after their son Charlie died of cholera at age seven. Catherine had always preferred city life to what tiny, bucolic Cassville offered. When daughter Katie left Stonefield to attend the University of Wisconsin, Catherine left her husband and joined her daughter in Madison, never to return. Their second son, Nelson Dunn, who was called Nettie, left Cassville to find his own way in the west. As with his mother,

Dewey, as an older man. WHI IMAGE ID 117520

it was a one-way trip. On top of such personal losses, Dewey suffered enormous financial losses in the national depression of the 1870s. As creditors closed in on his mortgaged holdings, his Stonefield mansion was gutted by fire.

He had his house rebuilt on a smaller scale as the two-story Victorian dwelling that can be found at the historic site today, but Dewey was hardly able to rebuild his life. For the next ten years he lived alone, seldom hearing from his estranged wife or children, and not at all in his last five years. When he served on the board of the new state prison at Waupun, he sometimes bunked at the prison to save money on lodging and had the prison tailor mend and press his suit.

It wasn't only his family that abandoned the former governor. When Dewey, then age seventy-three, traveled to Madison in 1887 to attend a reception for President Grover Cleveland, he was ignored at party headquarters, so he quietly left for home, alone again.

This was the final humiliation. Dewey never returned to Madison. In 1889 he suffered a stroke and five months later died in his room at the Denniston Hotel.

Stonefield was occupied for a time after Dewey's death but then stood empty for decades. In the 1930s, when the Newberry family that had owned the property decided to sell it, Cassville residents pushed for the creation of a state park named for Dewey, and about seven hundred acres were acquired by the state for that purpose. The house was restored, and in 1953 Stonefield was designated as the site of a state farm and craft museum, in part because of Dewey's life as a large-scale farmer. Today, the museum emphasizes agriculture and early rural life, including farm tools, tractors, threshing machines, and dairy equipment. Stonefield Village also features many re-created shops and businesses that would have been familiar to residents of all rural communities in southern Wisconsin in the 1800s.

PLACES OF INTEREST

~~Stonefield Historic Site, 12195 County Highway VV,~~ Cassville

Nelson Dewey State Park, 12190 County Highway VV, Cassville, features hiking trails and scenic views from five-hundred-foot Mississippi bluffs

The Cassville Car Ferry, the oldest operating ferry in the state of Wisconsin, runs from May into October, linking Cassville with Guttenberg, Iowa

5

Guttenberg's Misspelled Honor

The founders of Guttenberg, Iowa, seeded their new community on the Mississippi River with good intentions. In electing to honor Johannes Gutenberg, the famed inventor of movable-type printing, by naming their nascent community in his honor, the early German immigrants  here hoped to shine favorable attention on their countryman's great creation.

Then a funny thing happened. While early plats of the new Iowa community did indeed replicate the inventor's name to, well, a T, when city officials sent a second set of plats to G. A. Mengel Lithographing Company of Cincinnati, the artist who completed the work sent them back with the erroneous spelling of Guttenberg. And when no one objected, even after the mistake was recognized, the spelling stuck.

In faint fairness, research shows a number of spellings of the inventor's name in centuries-old records.

The man himself, however, "preferred the spelling 'Gutenberg,'" writes Walter W. Jacobs in his history of the town, *The First One Hundred Years*, "and the carelessness on the part of early city authorities in not adhering to the original spelling is, indeed, unfortunate, for the idea of naming a community after a man so eminent, and then dishonoring his memory by perpetuating his name with improper spelling, is so inconsistent that it has excited comment in the press over the nation."

At least old Johannes never knew of the slight. He died in 1468.

Germans were not the first to make a home at this spot along the river, nor was Guttenberg the first name used. Sac and Fox Indians had long spent summers in the area before the first white settlers arrived, and early French explorers called the area Prairie la Porte, or "door to the prairie." At first Prairie la Porte was merely a place for the sprawling District of Clayton County to hold court—a small tavern served as temporary courthouse— but in 1839 a part of the area along the river was surveyed and streets were laid out. The discovery of iron ore nearby brought a few speculative settlers, but the community was truly born when, in 1844, the Western Settlement Society of Cincinnati, an organization founded to aid German immigration, bought hundreds of acres in order to establish a strictly German community.

A convoy of ten steamboats and twenty-seven barges carrying a large group of German families left Cincinnati for Guttenberg in early February 1845. But the journey was so long and arduous that when the expedition reached Burlington, Iowa, most of the immigrants decided they had traveled far enough. Only five families continued the trek upriver to establish the new community.

"And what did they find when they arrived?" Jacobs wrote. "Very little," only the ruins of an old tavern and a few other county buildings. But eventually more of their countrymen arrived and a town was built—and promptly named after the famed inventor. The German influence was strong and obvious. Not all the local streets were given old-country names—Main, China, and Pearl, for example—but the motherland was given her due. Some streets were named for German thinkers like Goethe, Schiller, Lessing, and Wieland, and others for esteemed composers such as Mozart and Haydn. Even better, all the street names were spelled correctly.

Curiously, despite the five founding German families, the first mayor elected was an American who later served as the city's postmaster and historian. "The German mind," Jacobs concluded, "is not absorbed in the lust for office."

In time, Guttenberg became a pivotal place on the river, the "most important town between Dubuque and Prairie du Chien," Jacobs wrote. For a time it was the county seat of Clayton County (through a series of elections, nearby Elkader eventually wrested the courthouse away, lost it to Guttenberg, and finally claimed it for good), and the new community enjoyed boom years. Since its founding in 1851, the Iowa *Gazetteer* wrote in 1865, "The growth of this town has been both upward and rapid." Buildings of locally quarried stone, many still standing, gave the city a

A ferry boat at shore. WHI IMAGE ID 90626

handsome appearance, and its setting directly upon several miles of riverfront indelibly linked the community and its river. A ferry boat joined Guttenberg with Glen Haven on the Wisconsin side, businesses prospered along the riverfront, steamboats on the Mississippi brought goods and visitors from far and near, and emerging social and fraternal organizations added vibrancy to community life.

An action by one of those groups, the all-women Ingleside Club that formed in 1902, helped give Guttenberg the tourist-appealing look it retains today. Instead of electing a more conventional first project such as starting a library, the group chose instead to develop Ingleside Park along the river and raise money for its long-term upkeep. Today Guttenberg boasts a two-mile-long park and walking trail along a levee lined with dozens of river-facing benches that beckon visitors to relax and savor Old Man River's scenic delights—including, in winter months, a large number of bald eagles feeding in the open water.

Another signature improvement in 1903 was marked with merrymaking and music. After much effort to establish a power plant for the city, a whistle on October 23, 1903, signaled that the moment had come, and residents who rushed to their windows found their town entirely illuminated. As the headline in the *Guttenberg Press* declared, "And there is Light," Jacobs wrote, and none too soon, either, because "We have been stumbling around in the dark, with here and there an occasional oil lamp dimly burning."

To welcome the moment, the city band played under each light cluster in the business district that first bright night.

The years between 1910 and the advent of the first world war "were years of easy living in Guttenberg," Jacobs wrote, with full employment in local button factories, increased river traffic, and an active social life for those who sought it. But the impending war created divisions in Guttenberg, which had certainly not cast off its German connections. Some older residents who had been born in the old country held sympathy for Germany and its allies, which led to "many strong words and arguments" with neighbors who had no such sympathies. So bitter was the debate that after America's entrance into the war, residents presented the city council with a petition to change the town's name because of its German origin. The debate was similar to that in other towns with a strong German heritage, but eventually in Guttenberg the original name stuck.

Like many river towns, Guttenberg witnessed numerous efforts by shipping interests to tame the often-unruly Mississippi. In 1907 the US Congress approved a project to develop a six-foot-deep channel on the Mississippi, from the Missouri River to Minneapolis, accomplished by dredging the soil and constructing wing dams to contract the flow of water. Wing dams, or dikes, were underwater structures that reached partway into the river to

Harvesting ice on the Mississippi. WHI IMAGE ID 25848

The Lawler Bridge is another example of how humans tamed the river for travel and transport. Prior to the construction of this bridge in Prairie du Chien in 1874, railroad cars had to be towed across the river on barges.
WHI IMAGE ID 24811

force water into a fast-moving center channel more favorable for shipping. Dredging was a summer project, but men and horses built the dams in winter by dragging long bundles of willows onto the ice at selected locations, adding rock from local quarries, and dropping them to the river floor by cutting ice on either side. Wing dam construction kept hundreds of men busy during winters when other work was stopped.

A far more significant river project came in the 1930s when the US Army Corps of Engineers began building a system of locks

and dams that would offer a minimum channel depth of nine feet, better for shipping large quantities of goods on river barges. Dam No. 10 was planned for somewhere between Clayton, Iowa, and Cassville, Wisconsin, and the ultimate site chosen was smack in the middle of downtown Guttenberg. Because of high unemployment during the Depression years, officials decided to begin construction in 1934 as part of federal public works programs.

Construction of the lock and dam and cleanup of the river took three years, cost more than $3.8 million, and permanently changed both the river and the town. Dam No. 10 runs 6,510 feet in length and provides an eight-foot drop in the river between the upper and lower pools. More than four hundred people moved to Guttenberg to work on the dam's construction; many stayed after it was done, further diversifying the once mostly German community.

As it happened, the lock and dam also became a draw for short-term visitors. Of the twenty-nine such structures along the Mississippi, Lock and Dam No. 10 in Guttenberg was the best situated for tourists to see and enjoy. Downtown merchants benefited from the start, and the decision by the early ladies' club to establish a riverfront park proved prescient. For three days in 1937, Guttenberg observed both the hundredth anniversary of its founding as well as the dedication of Lock and Dam No. 10 with celebratory events Jacobs called "the finest displayed in the community either before or since." Men grew beards to be part of the Whisker Club, the high school gymnasium became a temporary museum, vintage German costumes were brought out from storage, "and for three glorious days Guttenberg was as a page from the past."

One eagerly awaited event was the "Mingling of the Waters," in which water from the headwaters of the Mississippi River and the Gulf of Mexico were to be combined. And it happened, if in a humorous manner. The mayor of New Orleans sent a century-old glass decanter of water from the gulf by special delivery airmail, requiring $7.69 postage due.

The water from Bena, Minnesota, arrived in a beer can, mailed with just eight cents' postage.

The house built for the lockmaster still stands—the last of its kind along the Upper Mississippi, now on the National Register of Historic Places. Today it welcomes visitors as a museum of early community history, operated by the Guttenberg Historical Society. The Federal Fish Hatchery built on the site in 1938, including an aquarium for freshwater fish species, still lures interested residents and visitors.

Despite the unfortunate misspelling of his name, Johannes Gutenberg is yet remembered and honored in Guttenberg. A two-volume facsimile copy of the Gutenberg Bible, printed at Leipzig, Germany, in 1913 and purchased from the Gutenberg Museum in Mainz, Germany, in the 1940s, sits on prominent display at the Guttenberg Public Library, where those who come to see it are invited to sign their names in a register.

Given the chance in 1949 to redress their early error, Guttenberg residents voted to stick with the misspelling. They voted 127 to 88 to leave bad enough alone, to Jacobs's continued dismay.

"To their eternal shame," he wrote, "the voters chose to follow the uninformed prophets who stirred up the public by untruthful statements that all deeds, abstracts and other instruments of record would have to be legally changed immediately."

And so the father of movable type is forever remembered by a typo.

PLACES OF INTEREST

An observation platform at Lock and Dam No. 10 allows visitors to watch barges and pleasure boats locking in on their journeys north and south. The Lockmaster's House Heritage Museum, just behind the observation deck, is open daily from May through August and weekends during September.

The Fish Aquarium and Hatchery, 331 S. River Park Drive, Guttenberg, now operated by the Iowa Department of Natural Resources, is open from May 1 through Oct. 1. www.iowadnr.gov/InsideDNR/ DNRStaffOffices/FishHatcheries/GuttenburgFish-Hatchery.aspx

Guttenberg's annual GermanFest, celebrating the community's heritage, is held the fourth weekend of September, during the peak of fall foliage. German music, folk dancing, and other activities take place in the historic downtown.

Other information can be found at www.guttenberg iowa.net/

6

A Scotsman on the River

Communities up and down the
Mississippi come with all manner of
self-proclaimed distinctions, from
smallest to longest, oldest to most
friendly. Winona, for example, calls
itself the stained-glass capital of the
United States, while Galesburg's
claim to fame was getting mistaken
for the Garden of Eden.

Only one river town, however, comes with links to Scotland's
most famous clan and, on top of that, was the birthplace of the
greatest show on earth. Visitors today can debate which city is the
friendliest, but McGregor, Iowa, is one of a kind.

If cities had official colors, McGregor's would be tartan. It was
named for, if not exactly spelled like, Alexander MacGregor, the
grandson of Scottish immigrants who left their homeland to escape persecution of their famous clan, which had been outlawed
for its opposition to British rule. (Think *Braveheart*.) The Mac-
Gregors initially lived in New York but various family members
eventually drifted westward, including Alexander, who moved to
the Mississippi River valley in 1835.

McGregor, Iowa, ca. 1906. WHI IMAGE ID 24280

By then, the end of the Black Hawk War had opened the region to an influx of new settlers, soldiers, trappers, and traders. All of these new arrivals had to cross the river somehow, so in 1837 MacGregor established a ferry across the Mississippi from busy Prairie du Chien. His first craft was small, a flatboard propelled by oars. As traffic increased, he had a larger ferry built, called the *Rob Roy MacGregor*, which was powered by four mules or horses that walked in a circular wheel in the middle of the boat. While that sounds odd in these engine-centric times, horse ferries were common in North America in those days, powering transportation on water as on land.

At first what was known as MacGregor's Landing was largely undeveloped, but MacGregor acquired more land and in 1846 a town was platted. When the town incorporated, residents dropped the "a" in favor of McGregor (apparently with the

family's consent). By 1857 the community was home to almost two hundred people, squeezed between the Mississippi and its soaring riverside bluffs.

More growth came after the Milwaukee and Mississippi Railroad finished laying track connecting the two waters. McGregor quickly became a significant commercial center, especially for shipping grain from Iowa and Minnesota across the river to destinations to the east. The nearby city of North McGregor—it would change its name to Marquette in 1920—became a large railroad terminus, but McGregor remained a major player in the grain business.

Again, the ferry business proved lucrative. Trains coming from the west carrying grain or other commodities would be disassembled at McGregor so cars could be ferried across the river one by one, then reassembled on the Wisconsin side for travel further east. So great was the business that by the 1870s, when 20 of the community's 120 businesses were connected to shipping or receiving grain or goods, McGregor's population exceeded five thousand. Today the business district of McGregor, which is listed on the National Register of Historic Places, still boasts many of the buildings constructed during those boom years, giving modern McGregor a genuine throwback appearance.

Few booms last forever, of course. In 1874, Prairie du Chien businessman John Lawler commissioned the construction of a pontoon bridge across the Mississippi to connect the railroad lines, eliminating the need to uncouple, ferry, and reassemble cars. At the time, according to the Marquette Depot Museum, it was the longest bridge of its kind in the world. In 1932 a suspension bridge for cars was built over the Mississippi, and in 1974 it was replaced by the Marquette-Joliet Memorial Bridge, a soaring link between two states that share the same river. The suspension bridge was closed two hours after the dedication of the new memorial bridge and was removed the following year. McGregor has always been a place of constant crossings, but as jobs were lost to such technological improvements the population began to shrink. Today the community of fewer than one thousand residents is solidly engaged in the business of tourism, known for its historic architecture, antique and specialty shops, and other activities.

Alexander MacGregor resided in the town of McGregor until his death in 1858. He was said to have owned a genuine clan seal inscribed, by one interpretation, "I am of royal descent/Slay and spare not," and a signet from Loch Lomond. And while Mac-Gregor became a successful businessman and landowner, he also was forced to endure a lengthy family feud and legal battle with his brother, James Jr., who claimed fraud over a land deal and sued his brother, inciting a twenty-year court battle finally resolved by an exchange of lots. When MacGregor died after a long illness, the town's founder was given rites appropriate for a descendant of royalty. One newspaper reported, "His funeral was the most imposing tribute of regard on the part of the citizens ever paid to a deceased fellow citizen in this part of the state. The cortege was half a mile in length numbering 50 to 75 teams carrying nearly a thousand people."

MacGregor was first buried behind his home in an area known as "The Heights," where his infant son had also been interred. However, after the feud settlement gave ownership of the property to James, Alexander's wife had her husband and son brought to Evergreen Cemetery in Prairie du Chien and reburied. In 2014, Scotland's Clan Gregor Society granted the town of McGregor, Iowa, "honorary" membership, in Alexander's memory.

～

McGregor's three-ring connections date to the community's early decades. In 1860 a harness maker named August Ringling moved to McGregor with his wife and three sons. August had changed his name from Rungeling after arriving in Milwaukee from Hanover, Germany. In McGregor, August developed a reputation for his skills with harnesses, saddles, and other leather goods. By 1874, after working in another man's harness shop, Ringling ran his own shop, where a newspaper ad claimed, "A. Ringling, halfway up Main Street, is turning out some of the handsomest as well as the most substantial harnesses that McGregor citizens or visitors ever looked upon or used."

August and his French-born wife, Salome, had four more sons. The struggle to make ends meet was constant, and Ringling welcomed whatever business came through the door. One fated day the "Cannonball Juggler" of a visiting circus walked in, with need of a harness maker's magic to repair equipment used in his act. He was as exotic a customer as the Ringling boys could have ever imagined.

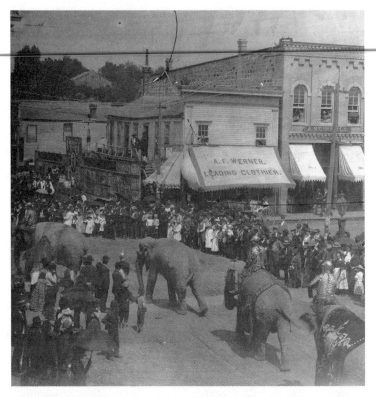

A large crowd watches elephants from the Ringling Brothers Circus walk through the streets of downtown Black River Falls. WHI IMAGE ID 101488

The boys had been smitten by the circus already. In *Ringlingville USA*, historian Jerry Apps describes the circuses that traveled through McGregor in the 1860s, including one that boasted "three great clowns," a "fully educated horse," and a balloon ascension that, tragically, resulted in the drowning of the balloon pilot when strong winds pushed his aircraft into the Mississippi River.

One of the Ringling sons, Alf T., later wrote of the big tent's lure for all the brothers: "It was a great day in the lives of these boys, who for two weeks had read and reread the crude posters on the walls of McGregor, which announced that on this particular morning a circus was coming to town."

The Cannonball Juggler paid his bill in circus tickets and left the boys forever possessed by circus fever. They began staging their own shows on Saturdays, first charging straight pins for admission (straight pins often were used as currency for people with no money, similar to playing poker with matchsticks) and later a penny a person. Their "wild animals" included cats, dogs, rabbits, and kittens and, one McGregor resident later remembered, a bullfrog with a sign that read, "Captured at great risk from the depths of a faraway swamp from which no other frog collector ever emerged alive."

"An old neglected white horse belonging to a man who lived nearby was the favorite with the Ringling boys," according to Apps's account, "and it was on its sway back they attempted their first 'bareback' riding."

By the 1870s a downturn in the harness business prompted August to relocate his family to Prairie du Chien, but the sons' interest in all things circus grew only stronger. By 1882, when the family had again moved to Baraboo, Wisconsin, the brothers were organizing a traveling show that eventually would become "the Greatest Show on Earth."

If Baraboo is the Ringlingville of Apps's title, McGregor's role in launching the Ringling brothers' circus dreams has not been forgotten. In 1996, all 875 residents of McGregor were invited as honored guests for the Ringling Bros. Barnum & Bailey Circus' 125th anniversary show in Des Moines, in tribute to those early backyard performances. The people of McGregor, a circus publicist explained, "feel such an ownership with the whole Ringling concept, understanding the spirit of what our performers do every day. To know we have a whole city in our state that understands that is truly magical."

PLACES OF INTEREST

McGregor Historical Museum, 256 Main Street, McGregor, open seasonally, www.mcgregor museum.org

Marquette Depot Museum, 216 Edgar St., Marquette

Pikes Peak State Park, 15316 Great River Road, McGregor, www.iowadnr.gov/Destinations/State ParksRecAreas/IowasStateParks/ParkDetails .aspx?ParkID=610141

7

Diamond Jo Reynolds

Every day, throngs of odds-ignoring optimists stream into the gleaming Diamond Jo Casino on Dubuque's Mississippi riverfront, borne on dreams of great fortune or, for the smaller group of realists who also take part, at least small hopes of bringing a penny slot machine to its knees.

Here's an irony, though. The man for whom the casino is named wasn't a gambler. He didn't even know how to gamble.

Diamond Jo Reynolds—"the Napoleon of the traffic on the upper Mississippi," one newspaper called him at the time of his death in 1891—wasn't a drinker or an utterer of oaths, either, but rather frugal and unpretentious. In fact, Reynolds was anything but the popular image of the steamboat man, but he nonetheless became the most successful and famous steamboat man of them all.

Joseph Reynolds was born in 1819, the youngest of six children in a Quaker family in Fallsburg, New York. Even in his youth he exhibited a businessman's acumen. On one occasion he accompanied his brother Silas to a general militia muster where

Silas intended to make money by selling ginger cakes. When Silas started calling "Cakes for sale!" another vendor attempted to out-shout him, which prompted young Joseph to seize the moment. "That man's cakes are good but these are better," he declared. "Good and better! Good and better!"

Years later, it could have been said of his steamboats as well. Reynolds tried his hand at various businesses in his youth, including butchering, flour milling, and tanning. After his marriage to Mary Morton in 1855, the couple moved west in search of new opportunities, establishing a tannery in Chicago and scouring Wisconsin, Iowa, and Minnesota for the hides to keep it operating. But it was his career change to wheat dealer that finally brought him to the Mississippi River, where he established a base in the community of McGregor, then a major wheat market.

He entered the boat business more by accident of necessity than by intent. Frustrated when other boat owners delayed his grain shipments or refused them entirely, Reynolds in 1862 arranged to have built the steamboat *Lansing*, a 123-ton stern-wheel boat that ran between Lansing, Iowa, and Prairie du Chien, Wisconsin. He followed that with the 242-ton *Diamond Jo* steamer and two grain barges. Reynolds left the boat business for a time, but when he worried another owner of a fleet of passenger and cargo ships was developing a monopoly that would limit his ability to ship grain, he jumped back in. This was the beginning of the Diamond Jo Line, a fleet of steamers and barges that came to dominate the grain trade on the Upper Mississippi.

People often wondered how Reynolds got his colorful nickname, and when answers proved elusive, they sometimes made up their own. In a letter to the editor of the *Winona Independent* in 1913, his friend O. K. Jones dismissed the theory that Reynolds got his nickname from a misshapen leg that, when he was standing, appeared to create a diamond-shaped space. The story, Jones said, was invented by a cabin boy in response to a passenger's

The *Diamond Jo* steamboat, docked at La Crosse in 1875, being loaded with goods for transport. WHI IMAGE ID 48622

question. "The boy did not know but a steamboat man in any capacity rarely owned to ignorance on any subject so the boy gave the reason as quoted," Jones wrote.

Others thought the name came from the impossible-to-miss diamond in Reynolds's lapel, which along with the noticeable ring on his hand prompted stories that he dealt in diamonds as well as wheat. Reynolds denied trading in gems.

"Never in my life," he once told a newspaper writer, "and I know very little about them. I bought this (lapel) stone from a poor fellow who needed the money. I gave him more money than he asked me for it, and this ring I bought from a man who wanted me to sell it for him. I could never get what he wanted for it, so I bought it myself. They tell a heap of things about me that never happened."

What did happen was this: In his early grain-trading days, Reynolds addressed his shipments to himself as J. Reynolds. When it turned out there was another J. Reynolds in the business he began using his nickname of Jo, along with marks on each side that resembled a diamond. The name stood out and became known up and down the river. Reynolds shipped a lot of grain in cotton bags, and when he had a hard time getting them returned he had them marked in large letters STOLEN FROM DIAMOND JO, to lessen the impulse to use them in making clothing.

In its early years, the Diamond Jo Line concentrated on grain shipping but after about 1880 became more involved in shipping freight and passengers. Ads for the line warned travelers to "avoid the discomforts of railroad travel," and his steamers became known for their considerable creature comforts. On Diamond Jo Line steamers, the *Dubuque Telegraph-Herald* reported, "A good orchestra is on each steamer and the meals are all that could be desired. No trip on the western waters to equal it." True to his Quaker roots, however, Reynolds's steamers lacked bars, and liquor was not served.

The *Muscatine Journal* reported the Diamond Jo steamer *Dubuque*, which ran between St. Louis and Burlington, Iowa, was known as "the honeymoon" craft, "owing to the fact that on nearly every trip she pulls out of St. Louis she has newly married couples as round-trip passengers. The last trip to Burlington . . . she had five bridal couples aboard. Chief Clerk George Pennover of the *Dubuque* states that one porter is kept busy nearly all the time clearing the decks of the rice which is showered upon the couples by their friends."

In later years Reynolds mused about building a line of even more palatial boats to reap the bounty of an increasing leisure class. After an interview with Reynolds in 1890, the *Clinton Weekly* told its readers, "The palmy days of travel on the Mississippi, he said, have yet to come. People travel on the river now for pleasure and pleasure travel is sure to grow. You couldn't carry a businessman from Dubuque to St. Paul by steamer if you were to offer him free transportation. Time is an important consideration for him. On the other hand, people who travel for pleasure care little for time but want all the elegance and comfort obtained. The line of elegant packets is bound to come in response to this demand."

An example of a packet ship. WHI IMAGE ID 48629

Reynolds, however, turned his attention to other pursuits. Suffering from various afflictions throughout his life, he frequently visited the medicinal waters of Hot Springs, Arkansas. He did not relish the long stagecoach ride required to reach the springs, and when his complaint that the service was a disgrace fell on deaf ears ("Ef yer don't like this ere kerrege," was the driver's reported reply, "w'at yer goin' to do about it?") he built the twenty-two-mile Hot Springs railway in 1875. The huge investment paid off, for Reynolds as well as those coming to take the cure at Hot Springs.

Later, Reynolds and his only son, Blake, became involved in gold and silver mining in Arizona and Colorado, an enterprise that eventually succeeded but not without a significant stumble. Their first purchase, of the Del Pasco mine in Arizona, was a costly error; it had been "salted" by previous owners to appear richer than it was, but the losses incurred there only prompted Reynolds to press on. His Congress mine, purchased in 1887 for $30,000, became one of Arizona's biggest producers.

It was while visiting that mine in 1891 that Reynolds took sick and died, leaving behind a fortune estimated at $7 million, a vast sum for the times. Even if the value of his estate shrank after his death, the *Clinton Weekly Age* noted, "there was sufficient left to make his widow one of the wealthiest women in Iowa." In memory of their son, Blake, who had died about a year earlier, the Reynoldses bequeathed money for a memorial park and fountain in McGregor and an endowment to the then-nascent University of Chicago. It was used to construct the Reynolds Club, still in use today as the student union.

Unlike some modern moguls, Reynolds never sought the attention that inevitably came to someone so wealthy and significant. In reporting his death, the *Dubuque Daily Herald* said the man with the flashy nickname instead "talked very little, shunned society, minded his own business very actively and, as he himself once put it, 'expected other people to do the same.'"

Not that they did. In the same interview in which Reynolds denied ever dealing in diamonds, he expressed frustration with those who would pile so much myth on a man they didn't know.

"They used to say that I swore like a trooper, dressed like a dandy, gambled, smoked, chewed tobacco and drank whisky by the quart. I don't do none of the things, except once in a great while I might go off to myself and very carefully say '_____ it,' but I don't know how to gamble. I never smoked or chewed. I haven't taken a drink of beer or whisky in twenty-five years. I wish people would let me alone. If you ever write anything about me nine-tenths of it won't be true and the other tenth won't be worth reading."

PLACES OF INTEREST

National Mississippi River Museum & Aquarium, 350 E. 3rd St., Dubuque, where Diamond Jo Reynolds is in the National Rivers Hall of Fame, www.rivermuseum .com

McGregor Historical Museum, 256 Main St., Mc-Gregor, www.mcgregormuseum.org

8

Zebulon Pike and His Peak

What's in a name? Often, clues to the past.

No explorer of today's Mississippi River should miss Pikes Peak—not the more famous site with that name in Colorado, but the dramatic promontory at McGregor, Iowa, arguably the most fetching spot on a river aflood with scenic wonders.

From atop the five-hundred-foot bluff, look to the north, at the suspension bridges linking Wisconsin and Iowa across the broad water and, in season, boats and barges at work and play. Look a bit south to where the Wisconsin River marries the Mississippi, the confluence first paddled by the Jesuit priest James Marquette and explorer Louis Joliet in 1673, and the green walls of Wyalusing State Park on the other side. If your timing is right, the mournful music of freight train horns on the Wisconsin riverside will serve as the soundtrack for your visit.

Then, imagine a fort on this very spot, as the explorer Zebulon Pike did when he arrived at this "most salubrious" place in 1805 on the first true American exploration of the Upper Mississippi Valley. In reality, the site would have been too difficult to supply

A steel-engraved portrait
of Zebulon Pike.
WHI IMAGE ID 89205

and might have allowed enemies to isolate a fort on the bluff's edge. The government agreed the site was wrong but approved the vicinity, so a fort was built instead across the river on the flat land at Prairie du Chien. But the site, now Iowa's Pikes Peak State Park, would carry the young explorer's name long after his visit, not the first land feature to carry Pike's name forever and far from the last.

Zebulon Montgomery Pike was just twenty-six years old when he and a twenty-soldier force left St. Louis on their expedition to the Upper Mississippi, charged with scouting suitable locations for military installations and with trying to turn Indians from their loyalty to the British, who then dominated the fur trade, and convert them to American allies instead. Unlike Lewis and Clark, who had left St. Louis one year earlier on their own exploration of the Upper Missouri, Pike was not sent with the blessings of President Jefferson but was sent instead by General James Wilkinson, a controversial figure who was later discovered to have been working in cahoots with Spain against the interests of his own government.

The hard-charging Pike likely cared little about Wilkinson's motivations as long as they advanced Pike's already considerable ambitions. The journey up the river, however, advanced slowly.

"In all cases," Paul Schneider wrote in *Old Man River: The Mississippi River in North American History*, "moving a boat upstream on the Mississippi without the benefit of steam power was backbreaking, soul-breaking, foot-rotting, snake-biting, fever-inducing, highly dangerous, low-paid work." But Pike, Schneider said, "was brave, perhaps fearless, ready to walk until his feet bled," and he demanded the same from his men, however much discomfort it caused them. The soldiers had to drag their keelboat over sandbars or cut it loose when snagged on logs, but Pike pushed his men hard, sometimes progressing up to thirty miles daily, and eventually reached the meeting of the two rivers.

"When they reached the mouth of the Wisconsin River," Biloine Whiting Young wrote in *River of Conflict, River of Dreams*, "they climbed the hill and planted the first American flag raised in the Northwest Territory."

Pike's contingent then headed north again, but only after trading their keelboat for somewhat more maneuverable flat-bottomed

bateaus. Where the Minnesota River met the Mississippi, he held
council with Indians at a place later named Pike Island. Young
wrote, "When the speech-making and ritual smoking of pipes
ended, Pike obtained from the Indians two pieces of land, one
on each side of the Mississippi River.

"The [Dakota] gave up these two parcels of land for an initial payment of sixty gallons of whiskey and trade goods worth
about $200. Since the treaty stipulated that the Indians could
go on using the land as they had in the past many, quite rightly,
got the idea they were agreeing to *share* the land with the white
settlers—not give it up entirely. Pike's was the first U.S. treaty to
be signed west of the Mississippi River."

And of course also that first treaty took far more than it gave.
One report called the whiskey "well-watered," a shamefully small
price to pay for land that would eventually become the cities of
Minneapolis and St. Paul, as well as the location of Fort Snelling.

Despite winter's encroachment Pike again pushed his men
north to a site near Leech Lake, where they established Fort Pike
as their winter refuge. Pike later wrote in his journal, "I will not
attempt to describe my feeling on my accomplishment of my
voyage, this being the main source of the Mississippi."

It was good that he saved the energy, given that the main source
of the Mississippi was actually several miles away at Lake Itasca.
But Pike, in addition to allowing his name to linger after his foot-
steps, was not above taking credit for great things. "In the execu-
tion of this voyage I had no gentleman to aid me," he wrote in the
summary report of his trip, "and I literally performed the duties
(as far as my limited abilities permitted) of astronomer, surveyor,
commanding officer, clerk, spy, guide and hunter; frequently pre-
ceding the party for miles in order to reconnoiter and returning
in the evening hungry and fatigued, to sit down in the open air, by
firelight, to copy the notes and plot the courses of the day."

Pike was certainly not without lasting accomplishments. In addition to choosing the site for Fort Snelling he also selected a site several hundred miles to the south on an island he called Big Island (Pike Island having already been taken), which became the city of Rock Island. And on his trip west on another journey of exploration, Pike tried, but failed, to climb the Colorado peak that nonetheless later was named for him.

Oddly, according to Young, Pike had known that promontory as Grand Peak. Those were only a few of the places to which his name became attached, which is especially noteworthy given that he died in an explosion during the War of 1812 at just thirty-four.

Iowa historian William J. Petersen wrote, "In pioneer days Pike's portrait was frequently displayed in frontier taverns. The first steamboat to reach St. Louis was appropriately named in his honor. Ten counties in as many states and eighteen towns and villages now bear his name, as do several bays, rivers and lakes. A number of states have erected monuments or plaques to his memory. Pike County Ballads were known from the banks of the Mississippi to the golden shores of California. Truly death did not blot out the memory of this intrepid soldier."

Who knows if it ever bothered Pike that his recommended fort site on top of the bluff was passed over for Prairie du Chien? But modern-day visitors can cheer the decision and enjoy the park developed there instead. The land was eventually owned by Alexander MacGregor, the founder of the nearby city of that name, who passed it on to a grand-niece. When she died her will directed that Pikes Peak, which she had never opened to settlers, be given as a gift to the federal government, which in turn conveyed the property to the state of Iowa. In 1935 it became a state park, a place of wondrous natural beauty, outdoor recreation, and rich river history.

PLACES OF INTEREST

Pikes Peak State Park, 15316 Great River Road, McGregor, Iowa, www.exploreiowaparks.com

National Mississippi River Museum & Aquarium, 350 E. 3rd St., Dubuque, where Pike is in the National Rivers Hall of Fame

Fort Snelling State Park, 101 Snelling Lake Rd., St. Paul, www.dnr.state.mn.us/state_parks/fort_snelling/index.html

9

A Most Historical Spot

If selling real estate is all about location, the same can be said about
selecting a place to settle. Throughout its history, Prairie du Chien was
selected early and often.

For centuries, Prairie du Chien
was a home and gathering place for
Indians from many tribes. Later, it

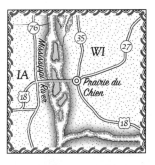

became Wisconsin's second-oldest city after Green Bay, and the
oldest settlement on the Upper Mississippi. For 150 years, Prairie du Chien was the center of fur trading on the river and was
variously controlled by the French, British, and Americans. And
it was the setting for Wisconsin's only major conflict in the War
of 1812.

The first white men who came to Prairie du Chien were the
famous explorers Marquette and Joliet in 1673, and they were
followed through the years by enough notable Americans to make
the city's story a veritable who's who. A frontier surgeon achieved
great advancements in medical knowledge in Prairie du Chien.
The key figure in Wisconsin's last Indian war surrendered here
to a future president of the United States, and a love story took

flight here (but didn't end well). In Prairie du Chien, history is a many-layered confection.

In 1952 the Wisconsin Historical Society established its first historic site in Prairie du Chien, opening the grand mansion known as Villa Louis to showcase nineteenth-century Victorian splendor.

In truth, though, the entire city is a historic site.

First, a word about that name. Many incorrectly surmise that Prairie du *Chien*—the French word for dog—was so named after prairie dogs, but there were none in Wisconsin. Instead, the name came from a Fox Indian chief named Alim, which meant *dog* in his native language. Various spellings were used by early traders and Indian agents, from La Prairie des Chiens to Prairie des Chiens, before the current name was agreed upon in the early 1800s.

But much had been going on long before that was settled. Less than a decade after Marquette and Joliet's exploration of the confluence of the Mississippi and Wisconsin Rivers, French

A fur trader in a council teepee. WHI IMAGE ID 3775

traders arrived here to do business with the Indians. The area had long been a Fox Indian village, and each spring members of other tribes, some of whom were bitter enemies, gathered here as a neutral place of barter and council. "For a few weeks they forgot their differences to trade, feast, smoke peace pipes, look for spouses, celebrate and play games," wrote author Biloine Whiting Young. "The Indians put aside all intertribal enmity during this time."

French traders found eager customers for their ammunition, tools, cloth, and other goods. Their currency was furs, in huge demand at the time for beaver hats and other clothing items, and a river island called St. Feriole just offshore from Prairie du Chien became a key trading center. Trappers from throughout the Great Lakes region brought huge numbers of furs there for shipment on the river to markets in the East.

While Indians had for years dominated the fur trade, the French, British, and Americans fought to wrest control, reducing the Sauk, Ho-Chunk, and other tribes to mere players in an often-confusing game.

"The wars among the French, British and the colonists for control of North America brought about changes in ownership of Prairie du Chien with dizzying frequency," Young wrote in her book *River of Conflict, River of Dreams.* "The Indians had good reason to be confused."

While the French had been first to control the fur commerce in Prairie du Chien, eventually the British assumed dominance, which put the frontier community in the crossfire when the War of 1812 broke out between the United States and Great Britain. During the war, US and British troops clashed over control of the trade and the position on the river. Matters escalated in 1814 when William Clark and a contingent of 150 soldiers sailed upriver from St. Louis and established Fort Shelby on top of a large Indian mound on St. Feriole Island. A British force responded by sending nearly 650 men from Fort Mackinac on Mackinac Island,

The original site of Fort Crawford. WHI IMAGE ID 42291

Michigan, to Prairie du Chien, where after three days of siege the Americans surrendered.

The British who took over the fort changed its name to Fort McKay, but when the war ended in 1815 and they were forced to withdraw, they burned it to the ground. Recognizing the importance of asserting control over the Upper Mississippi, US forces quickly built Fort Crawford on the same site, and Prairie du Chien and its surrounding area continued its place as a center of trade, treaty making, and military life on the frontier.

It was at Fort Crawford in the winters of 1829 and 1830 that the experiments of Dr. William Beaumont, an army surgeon, changed medical understanding of the digestive system. A few years earlier, at Fort Mackinac in 1822, Beaumont had saved the life of a young trapper named Alexis Martin after Martin suffered a shotgun blast to his abdomen. Martin survived, but his wound never fully closed. This allowed Beaumont to view the activities in Martin's stomach. Over a period of years, and during his service at Fort Crawford, Beaumont analyzed Martin's stomach juices, eventually leading to his 1833 publication of his findings on the physiology of digestion.

One of the first commanders at Fort Crawford was Colonel Henry Leavenworth, whose name would later be given to Leavenworth, Kansas; Fort Leavenworth; and Leavenworth Prison. Next came Major Philip Kearney, who, despite losing his arm in battle, would go on to become famous for his valor in the Mexican War; he was suc-

William Beaumont. WHI IMAGE ID 91788

ceeded by a future US president, Colonel Zachary Taylor.

Taylor was commandant at Fort Crawford in 1832 when Black Hawk surrendered there at the end of the tragic and bloody Black Hawk War, after hundreds of his followers were slaughtered a short distance upriver. The Sauk chief was escorted to prison in St. Louis by one of Taylor's aides, a lieutenant named Jefferson Davis, who would later become president of the Confederate States of America.

When Davis returned from St. Louis, he began a courtship with Taylor's second daughter, Sarah Knox "Knoxie" Taylor, who had just arrived at Fort Crawford after attending school in Cincinnati. Knoxie was a wonderful dancer, according to historian Martinus Dyrud in one of his many accounts of early Prairie du Chien:

"She was gay . . . charming. Her figure was slim, her hands and feet petite. Crowning her head was a mass of brown, wavy hair, which she parted in the center and divided into four graceful curls which hung to her bosom. What a splendid match, Knox sparkling, lovely and loveable, beauxed by her tall, slender and distinguished lieutenant, who stood straight as an arrow."

Taylor, however, strongly opposed their relationship, objecting not so much to Davis as to the idea of his beloved daughter becoming an officer's wife. His older daughter had already married an army doctor, and Taylor knew of his own wife's fears when he was off fighting.

"I will be damned if another daughter of mine shall marry into the army," he said, according to Dyrud.

But Davis and Knoxie continued to meet on the sly. Davis considered challenging his commander to a duel, but instead he resigned from the army, thus eliminating Taylor's concerns. Finally, in 1835, Davis and Knoxie married in Louisville, Kentucky, at the home of Knoxie's aunt, Elizabeth Taylor. Tragically, however, Knoxie contracted malaria and passed away just three months later. Davis, who nearly died of the same disease, became so distraught he lived as a recluse for the next eight years.

In 1828, flooding at the original Fort Crawford created uninhabitable conditions, and a new fort was constructed on the mainland in Prairie du Chien. St. Feriole Island, however, continued to play a significant role in Prairie du Chien life. In the 1840s, fur trader and wealthy businessman Hercules Dousman made his home on the very Indian mound where the first fort had stood and began building a grand Victorian estate that would serve his family for three generations.

Dousman's son, H. Louis Dousman, built an impressive Victorian home there in 1870 and later established a prominent horse farm for breeding and racing trotting horses. When Louis died in 1886, the horses were sold, paddocks became fields, and the grand residence was named Villa Louis as a memorial to its builder. The home was later closed, but in the 1930s the family returned to create one of the first historic house museums in the Midwest. The property became Wisconsin's first state historic site

Hercules Dousman.
WHI IMAGE ID 112714

H. Louis Dousman.
WHI IMAGE ID 5392

Villa Louis, ca. 1960. WHI IMAGE ID 42005

in 1952, and in 1995 it underwent an extensive restoration to put a new shine on its 1890s appearance.

Today, after many of its early structures were moved to escape frequent floods, much of St. Feriole Island has been turned into park space. However, Villa Louis and three other buildings—the Fur Trade Museum, the 1837 Brisbois House, and the Dousman House Hotel—have been designated National Historic Landmarks and continue to reflect what life on the riverfront was like in Prairie du Chien's past.

PLACES OF INTEREST

Villa Louis, 521 N. Villa Louis Rd., Prairie du Chien, which also operates the Fur Trade Museum and Brisbois House, is open daily May–October. http://villalouis .wisconsinhistory.org/Visit/AdmissionsHours.aspx

Fort Crawford Museum, 717 S. Beaumont Rd., operated by the Prairie du Chien Historical Society, has exhibits on Dr. Beaumont and his experiments, the city's military history, fur trade days, and more. Open May–October. www.fortcrawfordmuseum.com/

Fort Crawford Cemetery Soldier's Lot, 413 S. Beaumont Street, is one of the nation's smallest military cemeteries with just over sixty graves. www.cem .va.gov/cems/lots/fort_crawford.asp

Cornelius Family Park & Tourist Information Center, on US Highway 18 at the base of the Marquette-Joliet Bridge, houses the regional tourism information center and features a 1910 statue of Father Marquette facing the Mississippi River he and Joliet explored.

Wyalusing State Park, ten miles south of Prairie du Chien at Bagley, boasts expansive views of the confluence of the Wisconsin and Mississippi Rivers. http:// dnr.wi.gov/topic/parks/name/wyalusing/

10

The Button Boom

In the late 1890s, pearl button fever swept through communities up and down the great river like an epidemic. In exploring the button boom along the Upper Mississippi, we could turn to academic examinations, and though we shall do some of that, more fun is to start with a  lively account straight from the button's mouth, "The Story of My Life by Billie Button."

Billie's autobiography, written "in true fifteen cent magazine fashion," was published in 1914 by the Wisconsin Pearl Button Company of La Crosse, a humorous but informative piece of early American marketing designed to explain the booming business of pearl button manufacturing and to boast of the company's role in shipping millions of buttons to clothing manufacturers across the land.

"My name is Billie Button," the account begins, "and my home is now at La Crosse, Wisconsin, but I expect to make a trip soon and where I'll end up Heaven only knows. On the waist of Sidney Christopher Sparks, at Punxsutawney, Pennsylvania, maybe, or perhaps bedecking the dress that little Lucille Dunwoody, of

Workers sitting on a large mound of empty clam shells at a pearl button factory in Prairie du Chien. WHI IMAGE ID 64420

Tulare, California, wears to her birthday party. Now I'm not a Kipling or an Ernest Seton-Thompson, but if you'll be patient and let me spin my yarn in my own way I think you'll find it interesting."

The button boom was interesting, all right, a "wild free-for-all" while it lasted, as the National Mississippi River Museum in Dubuque describes it. Pearl button fever made some men rich and others sorely disappointed, though it nearly depleted the freshwater clam stocks of the river.

Until the mid-nineteenth century, buttons were made from cloth, metal, bone, and ocean shells. It had long been known that various stretches of the Mississippi were home to millions and millions of freshwater mussels, or clams, but early efforts to use them in button manufacturing had found limited success, mostly because of a lack of capital and proper equipment.

Credit for turning clamming into a commercial success goes to a German turner and button maker named J. F. Boepple, who first encountered freshwater mussel shells when they were sent to his father in their hometown of Ottensen, Germany. Boepple believed the shells held great promise for button manufacturing, so he moved to the United States, where he farmed for a while in Illinois while scouting nearby rivers for rich mussel populations. Eventually Boepple's search took him to the Mississippi, where among other places he found especially abundant clam beds near Muscatine, Iowa.

Boepple began turning out buttons from the clamshells he gathered by hand and sold them to a Muscatine dry goods store. He then developed a device that trailed a number of hooks in the water and increased his haul. By 1891, after finally enticing investors, Boepple established the first freshwater pearl button factory at Muscatine, which in turn drew other button makers over the next few years. Soon Muscatine was known as the Pearl Button Capital of the World, with 2,500 people employed in more than forty button-related businesses.

The button boom was on. New machines came along to help convert clamshells into buttons, and the industry expanded to more than a dozen communities along the Mississippi and on

Men, women, and children living at a clam camp. WHI IMAGE ID 64431

other inland rivers. By 1898, more than a thousand clammers made their living off of mussel fishing, often living during the summer months in crowded clamming camps. Button factories, like the one in La Crosse where Billie Button's own conversion occurred, employed many hundreds more.

Of course, Billie couldn't tell her personal experience in the factory without first relating how clams with such inelegant nicknames as Slop Bucket and Pig Toe were wrenched from their comfortable life on the mud flats of the Mississippi and given the great responsibility of holding up Sidney Sparks's pants or young Lucy Dunwoody's party skirt. "[T]he clam's lot nowadays isn't such a soft snap after all," Billie wrote, "how it's worried and flurried, hunted and harried, and finally dragged from its bed to a slaughter of the innocents."

Billie described the "crow's foot" commonly used by clammers, an iron bar ten to fifteen feet long that trailed up to twenty strings with three-pronged hooks attached. Because clams rest in beds with their mouths open facing upstream, clammers could

A clammer on the Mississippi River removes his catch after dragging the line of hooks along the bottom of the riverbed. WHI IMAGE ID 64433

easily drag the hooks over a bed and, when pulled up, "most of the prongs on most of the hooks on most of the lines had a nice, fat clam hanging on for dear life."

"Farewell to the contented idleness of the family Clam Bed," Billie wrote. "Farewell to the generous feeding of the mighty river. My ancestor now becomes a martyr—not to SCIENCE but to commerce. When the clammers who caught him went ashore, they dumped their load into a big vat of water and built a hot enough fire under it to kill their catch; remorselessly, relentlessly and chuckling with unholy glee."

The boiling water allowed the clam's jaws to part so processors could check for pearls and pull out the meat that was later sold to neighboring farmers for hog feed. The shells were moved to the factory, where they were graded for color, luster, and breakage. Then they were sorted, soaked in water to make them tougher and less brittle, and cut into button shapes.

"And here is where my own life story really begins," Billie wrote. "I soon found out that however much HUMAN babies are coddled, baby BUTTONS have a perilous time of it."

Button blanks were passed through sorting machines and then into grinders—"severe kindergarten for infant buttons," Billie called it—to have shell "bark" smoothed off and rough edges softened. Next, the buttons were fed into another machine that cut depressions in the middle and then buttonholes, sometimes four and sometimes two.

"At last," wrote Billie, who was herself a four-holer, "I am a really unmistakable Pearl-Button," sewed onto a card with eleven identical buttons for shipment.

Beyond explaining the button business, the booklet helped to polish the reputation of the Wisconsin Pearl Button Company. The company employed 350 workers; used what was, at the time, cutting-edge equipment; and even had a small hospital ward on site to treat ill or injured workers and to offer preemployment

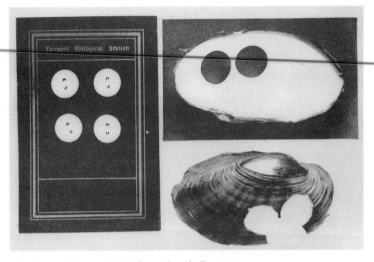

A package of buttons made from clamshell. WHI IMAGE ID 73164

screenings to female job applicants to ensure they were in physical condition to handle the work.

And there was plenty of work to go around. The company produced ten different sizes of buttons, with twelve different patterns in both two-hole and four-hole styles, and eight different grades. By 1907, the company produced 237,400 buttons a year, and more than 1,580,000 buttons six years later.

"We Pearl-Buttons, of the Fresh Water branch of the family, have worked a revolution in the button business," Billie boasted, to become "a power in the world's industrial life. Thirty-seven billion, five hundred million of us went forth from the button factories of America last year. What do you think of that?"

Like most booms, however, the button heyday eventually faced an inevitable bust. Over-clamming reduced the mussel population. Construction of locks and dams on the river changed the underwater environment, and pollution further took a toll on clam beds. In the 1920s, plastic buttons emerged as a cheaper and easier-to-manufacture alternative. By the 1930s many clamming

Workers inside a La Crosse button factory. WHI IMAGE ID 73186

areas were closed by regulators in hopes that beds would recover, but by 1940 commercial clamming had largely ended. In Muscatine, dozens of button-cutting shops closed, while a few manufacturers turned to plastic button making to stay in business.

If the industry's story ends more with a fizzle than with a bang, Billie's own story concludes on a high note.

> Here, patient reader, is my Epilogue, the thing the classy author always tacks on his story to dispose of his characters after the wedding bells and rice.
>
> I'm in the world at last—and how I traveled to get there! First to the big home of a jobbing house in Cincinnati, then (happily for my literary ambitions) out to a store in a little Indiana town. On then . . . to the dressmaker where snip, off the card I went, and skillful fingers sewed me fast to a little girl's frock. That's where I am now . . . and Isabel's mamma says I'm a mighty good Pearl-Button to stand the wear and tear of schooldays and washdays the way I do.

PLACES OF INTEREST

The Pearl Button Museum at Muscatine, Iowa, History and Industry Center, 117 W. Second St., www.muscatinehistory.org

The complete autobiography of Billie the Button can be found at www.wisconsinhistory.org/turning points/search.asp?id=1450

Many small museums along the river also have exhibits on the pearl button industry.

11

Treasure from the Mud

Most Mississippi River clammers prized mussels for the shells, which were sent off to nearby factories and turned into buttons. This left behind mountains of clam meat, often used by area farmers as hog feed.

But other clammers—whether heeding the biblical admonition not to cast pearls before swine, or simply because they were more practical—sought treasures far more valuable, and far less common, than mere button shells. This exclusive group of clammers sought Mississippi River pearls, and for a few decades in the early 1900s they turned pearl prospecting into a miniature version of gold prospecting in the west, with mud flats serving as this industry's rich, gold-flecked hills.

Natural pearls were especially valued in the days before cultured pearls were developed by a Japanese scientist around the turn of the century. They came in many colors, most commonly white and pink, but also bright blue or blood red. The pearl's shape was determined by its location in the shell. Blister pearls, which were attached to the shell and irregular in shape, were most

Clammers near Muscatine, Iowa. WHI IMAGE ID 73177

common, while those along the lip were more often round and
more valuable.

Only a small percentage of mussels contain natural pearls.
A good-sized irregular pearl can be found in about one of 100
clams, according to the Wisconsin Department of Natural Resources, while a good-sized round pearl appears only in one in
about 10,000 clams. Other estimates put the odds against such
valuable pearls even higher, but when clammers began hauling
mussels from the Mississippi by the millions during the button
boom, the chances were deemed good enough—and the potential reward rich enough— that large numbers of pearl hunters
eagerly joined the search.

Buttons to hold up a man's pants might fetch pennies, but
pearls lustrous enough to hang on a lady's ears or around her neck
left many a clammer dreaming in dollar signs. Many a clammer
beat the long odds and found their fortunes. Prairie du Chien
was a special hotbed for pearl prospectors and pearl buyers, who

would resell river pearls to jewelers in Chicago, New York, and beyond. At one time, according to researcher Eric Temte, "There were 27 pearl buyers registered in Prairie du Chien, people from India, France, England and various parts of the United States. In 1903 the town was known all over this county and Europe as the central mart of the American freshwater pearl."

Stories of clammers who hit it rich spread far and wide, ratcheting up interest in the river's hidden treasures. Some clammers in Prairie du Chien were said to have built homes from the sale of a single pearl, which could fetch as much as $1,000. Pearl fever

A 1901 advertisement for the Milwaukee-based Bunde and Upmeyer jewelry company boasts the use of Wisconsin pearls. WHI IMAGE ID 90409

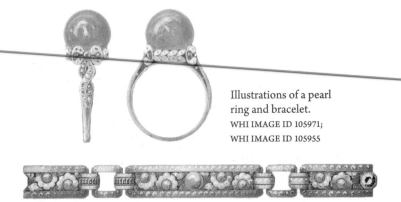

Illustrations of a pearl
ring and bracelet.
WHI IMAGE ID 105971;
WHI IMAGE ID 105955

became so rampant that hunters killed off mussels by the millions, according to the US Fish and Wildlife Service, eventually decimating entire mussel beds in parts of the Mississippi.

Local residents were among the pearl buyers. One local buyer, John Peacock, described buying a particularly spectacular pearl found by a clammer in an especially good pearl bed near Genoa, Wisconsin.

Late one night Peacock was summoned to a tavern in nearby Harpers Ferry, Iowa, where a customer was showing off a fine pearl he had found that day. The nut-sized gem measured fifteen-sixteenths of an inch in diameter. Peacock examined the pearl by lantern light—"It seemed all the colors of the rainbow danced in this gem" according to Temte's account—and bought it on the spot for $1,000. That same pearl was later purchased for $5,000 by a Chicago fine arts dealer, who in turn sold it for $10,000 to a New York buyer, who later sold it for twice that amount to a buyer in England. The Genoa Pearl, as it came to be called, was too big for use in jewelry, but it was coveted by collectors and eventually became part of the English royal family's crown jewel collection.

No wonder long odds couldn't wash away the high hopes among pearl hunters, even if not all success was strictly the fruit of hard work. There was also the story of a man in northeastern Iowa who bought some clam meat for catfish bait. After cleaning his catch, he threw the catfish innards to his chickens, but soon noticed a rooster having trouble digesting his meal. The problem, of course, was a "sizeable but battered and discolored pearl" that Peacock nonetheless bought for $150. When he peeled off the outer "skin" of the pearl, Temte wrote, Peacock discovered one of the rarest gems of his career, a pearl of "deep pigeon-red."

Pearl prospecting thrived from about 1890 until 1920, but by then the Japanese cultured pearl industry had diminished the market price of natural pearls, just as the over-harvesting of mussels from the Mississippi and other environmental factors reduced the number of button shell clammers. By 1939 only two pearl buyers remained in Prairie du Chien, and only a handful of local prospectors were left.

Today, a number of species of Mississippi mussels are considered threatened or endangered, and it is no longer legal to harvest live mussels from Wisconsin waters. Still, buyers and sellers of freshwater pearls that were harvested years ago can be found in sizable numbers with a quick internet search, and the value of such pearls is expected to increase as time goes on. A few jewelry makers along the Great River Road offer items made with freshwater pearls, including the Mississippi River Pearl Jewelry Company in Alma, which is said to have sold three pearls to the English royal family, one for use in jewelry for Queen Elizabeth and another that was set in a ring for Princess Diana. Owner Nadine Leo, who was one of the first artists along the river to work with Mississippi pearls, said she still has a good supply of natural pearls, in part because of clammers who only recently began selling pearls found years ago.

PLACES OF INTEREST

~~The Pearl Button Museum at Muscatine, Iowa, His-~~ tory and Industry Center, 117 W. Second St., www .muscatinehistory.org

Mississippi River Pearl Jewelry Company, 125 N. Main St., Alma, Wisconsin, www.mspearl.com

Many small museums along the river have pearl button exhibits, as does the National Mississippi River Museum & Aquarium, 350 E. 3rd St., Dubuque, www .rivermuseum.com

12

Effigy Mounds
and Eternal Mysteries

It takes some effort to get to the top, but the steep trails at Effigy Mounds National Monument just north of McGregor, Iowa, reward breathless visitors with some of the most magnificent views anywhere along the Upper Mississippi. From the prominent feature known as Hanging

Rock, you can look down at the great river and its forested hillsides. From the bluff called Fire Point, you can gaze as far south as Iowa's Pikes Peak State Park and across the water to Prairie du Chien, Wisconsin. The spot called Third Scenic View overlooks some of the river's countless islands, and of course the reward at Eagle Rock might well be a majestic bald eagle riding the wind.

The earthen shapes that line these trails may be less visually magnificent, but they're captivating in a more mysterious way, as the mounds, which were built as many as 1,400 years ago, are more about puzzles and possibilities than questions asked and answered.

Platform Mound, near Trempealeau. WHI IMAGE ID 114205

Why were these mounds—in the shapes of bears, birds, tur-
tles, and more—built by prehistoric people? Who was meant
to see them? What did they signify? Were they messages to the
people of the future, or merely monuments for the people of that
time? Why were some used for burials but not many more?

In a world in which so much is explained to travelers by guide-
books, maps, markers, and experts, perhaps a bit of mystery is
worth seeking out.

Effigy Mounds National Monument was established in 1949
by order of President Harry Truman, whose proclamation declared the site with its mysterious mounds "of great scientific
interest." The act came after almost forty years of debate, study, ar-
gument, and bureaucratic wrangling over proposals to establish a
national park along the Mississippi River. Proposals varied in size
and scope; the most grandiose would have created a wooded river
bluff park nearly 220 miles long, covering four counties in Iowa,
one in Illinois, four in Minnesota, and eight in Wisconsin. The

logistics for acquiring and operating such a massive park caused the effort to die of its own weight, but the proposal eventually led to the far more narrow effort to protect the prehistoric mounds area as a national monument.

Up and down the Mississippi Valley, early people now known as the Woodland Indians built thousands of effigy mounds, some as early as 2,500 years ago. The 206 mounds at Effigy Mounds National Monument were likely built between 850 and 1,400 years ago during the Late Woodland period and include thirty-four in the form of animals. The others are conical, or round domes of earth; linear, usually two to four feet high and stretching as many as 100 feet long; or a combination of conical and linear mounds joined together.

The largest at the monument is Great Bear Mound, 137 feet long and 70 feet wide at the shoulder, while the Marching Bear Group features ten smaller bear mounds and three bird mounds in a fairly tight cluster.

Another example of an effigy mound is Bear Effigy Mound at Lake Koshkonong, shown here with its contours outlined in chalk. WHI IMAGE ID 78519

A Ho-Chunk man in traditional Woodland dress. WHI IMAGE ID 62089

Why? And for what purpose? Is it significant, or just a coincidence, that most of the effigies were built facing downriver? Were the people who were buried in some of the mounds important figures being honored by their communities, or merely people who died when the mounds were being built?

If these early builders were trying to keep their motives secret, they did a lasting job. But limited excavations and studies have offered clues. Items found in excavated mounds include sewing needles made from bird bones, a copper breastplate, copper beads, and pieces of pottery. A small number of mounds were used as burial sites. Archaeologists believe the mounds may have been clan symbols, monuments, totems to animal spirits, or territorial markers. But educated guesses are still just that.

This much we know: The long struggle to create Effigy Mounds National Monument has preserved important places that otherwise may have been lost. Many other mounds were lost through the years when plows destroyed them, development swallowed them up, or rivers changed their minds and their directions and engulfed them. In the 1880s an archaeologist at Harpers Ferry, about ten miles to the north of the national monument, counted more than 900 mounds, but visitors today will find only one or two that have survived there.

Effigy Mounds National Monument is popular with hikers and draws thousands of visitors each year. But it is a spiritual site as well. In 2006, the Park Service erected a marker at the base of the Fire Point trail with a welcome from Chloris Lowe, a Ho-Chunk Indian leader, that included this reminder:

We ask that as you walk over this land to please remember
this is sacred ground to those of the mound building culture.
The descendants of this culture are not a lost people but
rather living, thriving American Indian cultures that today

reside in what is now called the Midwest. These native descendants continue to honor their ancestors buried here in religious ceremonies on these sacred sites. Please enjoy and respect your time among the "old ones" as their spirits will watch over you while you are here.

PLACES OF INTEREST

Effigy Mounds National Monument, 151 Hwy. 76, Harpers Ferry, Iowa, is four miles north of McGregor on Highway 76. www.nps.gov/efmo/index.htm

13

When the River Ran Red

The unincorporated community of Victory in western Wisconsin's Vernon County is a don't-blink-or-you'll-miss-it spot on the Great River Road, and the Mississippi explorer who simply drives through might think the name was inspired by a rousing moment in American history. Victory. How nice.

It was anything but that. If truth in advertising could be applied to place names, the sign would more honestly read "Massacre," for it was near this spot, where the Bad Axe River meets the Mississippi, that the last Indian war in Wisconsin ended in shamefully bloody fashion in the summer of 1832. And if truthfulness should apply to event names as well, the Battle of Bad Axe was not so much a battle as it was a slaughter.

The roots of what would become the Black Hawk War were planted in St. Louis in 1804 when certain chiefs and elders of the Sauk and Fox tribes entered into a treaty with the governor of the Indiana Territory, William Henry Harrison. Under the terms, the Indian elders agreed to relinquish nearly fifty million acres of land for about $2,500 and an annual payment of $1,000.

Site of the Battle of Bad Axe. WHI IMAGE ID 2531

Other Sauk chiefs who had not been part of the meeting decried the agreement, arguing those who had been there had no authority to speak for the Nation and that therefore the treaty was invalid. For nearly thirty years after the treaty was signed, the Indians continued to live in their village of Saukenuk, on the east side of the Mississippi near the mouth of the Rock River in the present-day Quad Cities.

Their leader Black Hawk was among those who viewed the treaty as invalid. He was not a hereditary chief or medicine man but instead a respected warrior and commander. In his autobiography, dictated in 1833 while in US custody after the war, Black Hawk argued that the four leaders who approved the St. Louis treaty "had been drunk the greater part of the time they were in St. Louis," and he criticized the paltry payment to the Sauk. "I could say much about this treaty, but I will not, at this time," he said. "It has been the origin of all our difficulties."

By 1829, lead fever made those difficulties untenable. Non-native settlers were pouring into the region to mine without caring about treaties or the land's legal owners. The Sauk, led by Chief Keokuk, complied with a US government order to move west of the Mississippi in return for a promise of sufficient corn to make it through the winter. But the government failed to keep its promise.

In the spring of 1832, the government's failure prompted Black Hawk and more than a thousand followers to return to their traditional homeland on the east side of the Mississippi in hopes of harvesting their own corn. While the move was certain to alarm white settlers, Black Hawk trusted that his Ho-Chunk neighbors would help defend the Sauk from any hostility from the Americans. Black Hawk also believed that the British forces to the north, for whom the Sauk and Fox had fought in the War of 1812, would be allies.

Black Hawk. WHI IMAGE ID 11706

Sadly, Black Hawk and his people found no such support and instead faced plenty of aggression. A hastily formed and woefully untrained unit from the Illinois militia set after Black Hawk, and on May 14, 1832, several hundred soldiers attacked Black Hawk and about forty of his men who had separated from the rest of their people. In the face of far superior numbers, Black Hawk chose to surrender, but the militia spurned his white flag in favor of opening fire.

"Never was I so much surprised in my life, as I was in this attack!" Black Hawk later said in his account. The Indian response was so ferocious that the militia hastily retreated and what became known as the Battle of Stillman's Run lit the match of war.

In truth, the war was more of a chase conducted over sixteen weeks as Black Hawk and his increasingly desperate people, including many women and young children, attempted to avoid being attacked while they struggled to make it back across the Mississippi River. Their flight took them through the lead region of Illinois and into Wisconsin, through the future site of Madison and up to the Wisconsin River near Sauk City. There, after a brief skirmish, soldiers thought they had the Sauk people cornered, only to learn the next morning their prey had slipped across the Wisconsin River under veil of darkness and were gone again.

Such Indian successes were limited, however. The Sauk people were without food or adequate water, and many young and very old members of their group died of starvation or exhaustion and were left along the trail.

Finally, on August 1, the beleaguered Sauk reached the bank of the Mississippi at the mouth of the Bad Axe River, where they were caught in crossfire between pursuing soldiers and a gunboat on the river.

Again, Black Hawk tried to surrender.

Again, the white flag was ignored.

An artist's rendition of the Battle of Bad Axe. WHI IMAGE ID 2466

As an account of the events by Robert B. Smith in *Military History* magazine described it, "It was all over now but for the killing." The steamboat *Warrior*, under the command of Captain Throckmorton, fired deadly cannon bursts from the water, while the army closed from behind. Some Indians successfully made it to the other side of the river only to be killed by their enemy, the Sioux, who had taken the side of the Americans. More than 150 Sauk warriors were killed that day, most then scalped by the soldiers. Many women and children who were not killed by grapeshot or rifle fire drowned, and those of Black Hawk's band who survived were taken prisoner.

Black Hawk was not among them. "He had left before the battle, old and tired and sick at heart," Smith wrote in *Military History*. "Whether he had simply given up on the war or was trying to lead part of [General] Atkinson's troops away from the Indian families is not clear. In any case, his people did not blame him for his absence. He had led them well. The long march was over. Black Hawk had lost."

Black Hawk remained elusive for more than three weeks until, on August 27, he and other Sauk leaders surrendered to army officials in Prairie du Chien. He was then taken "under the charge of a young war chief, who treated us all with much kindness." That young war chief was Lieutenant Jefferson Davis, the future leader of the Confederacy and just one notable figure from the time who played a part in the Black Hawk events. A young Abraham Lincoln spent a short, miserable stretch in the Illinois militia, while Colonel Zachary Taylor commanded the Fort Crawford garrison at Prairie du Chien.

Black Hawk was later taken on a highly publicized tour of the eastern United States, intended to impress upon him the fact that the Americans were too populous and too powerful to oppose. When he met Andrew Jackson, the "Great White Father," in Washington, Black Hawk recalled in his autobiography, "He said he wished to know the cause of my going to war against his white children. I thought he ought to have known this before; and, consequently, said but little to him about it—as I expected he knew as well as I could tell him."

Black Hawk died in 1838 at his new home in Iowa, where he was buried in the traditional manner—sitting up in a small mausoleum of logs. In a final insult, his grave was soon robbed. His remains were later taken to a museum in Burlington, Iowa, but were lost when the building burned in 1855.

In 1852 a fledgling community was born near the site of the sad slaughter of Black Hawk's people. It was named Victory by Judge William F. Terhune. Historians were not so rosy-eyed, though, almost universally condemning the actions of Throckmorton and the American soldiers. Historian Reuben Gold Thwaites declared the event "a massacre" in a speech at the battle site in 1898, a conviction shared by others who examined the bloody end of the so-called war.

An undated photograph of the town of Victory. WHI IMAGE ID 100819

A series of roadside historical markers document Black Hawk's flight through Illinois and Wisconsin, including one near the battle site dedicated by Thwaites in the 1930s. It informs those curious enough to slow their journey on the Great River Road that "Of the 1,000 Sacs who crossed the river from Iowa in April 1832, not more than 150 survived to tell the tragic story of the Black Hawk War."

Moreover, as Stephen Ambrose and Douglas Brinkley wrote in their book *The Mississippi and the Making of a Nation*, "Although Bad Axe is little known, more Indians died there than at the famous massacres at Washita, Sand Creek or Wounded Knee."

In 1989, at a time when relations between state officials and Indian bands in northern Wisconsin were strained by disagreements over treaty rights, the Wisconsin Legislature passed a resolution formally apologizing for the actions of American troops at the Bad Axe River.

PLACES OF INTEREST

Black Hawk Park, on Battle Island where the final
fighting of the Battle of Bad Axe occurred, also offers
camping, hiking, boat launches, and other activities.
It is operated by the US Army Corps of Engineers.

The Hauberg Indian Museum, which interprets the
story of the Sauk and Meskwaki Indians, and Black
Hawk State Historic Site are at 1510 46th Ave. in Rock
Island, Illinois. www.blackhawkpark.org/museum

14

Steamboats on the River

One of the truly delightful throw-backs along the Mississippi River can be found at the levee in La Crosse's Riverside Park when the largest steamboat ever built docks for a few hours on its nine-day cruise between St. Louis and St. Paul. To watch the *American Queen* with its tall stacks  spewing steam, to hear its calliope's song, to see its decks lined with passengers eager to disembark and the bank of the river lined with greeters, some in vintage clothing, is to experience—for just a few hours—what river towns long knew as a way of life.

Steamboats came, and steamboats went.

The river was always a highway. Native Americans used long birch bark canoes to navigate the Mississippi, and the French Canadians who came to trade with them adopted such crafts as well. Later, as more settlers moved west, flat-bottomed rafts were used to transport people and their household belongings—which could include cows and chickens, of course—but that convey-ance came with severe limitations. Because of the river's strong current, rafts could easily enough go south, but working back

A steamboat travels along the Mississippi River, near Indian Mounds Park in St. Paul. WHI IMAGE ID 68756

upriver was so difficult that rafts were often broken up for their wood upon arrival in the south. People returning north would go on foot.

Larger flatboats followed, often poled with long oars by as many as ten men. These keelboats could go upriver, but they often required men on shore pulling with ropes to make real progress. Still, it meant traffic could go in two directions on the Upper Mississippi, and there certainly was demand for such transportation.

"Adventurers, soldiers, tourists, settlers—the assorted denizens of the American frontier—rode the keelboats on their torturous journey upriver into the Northwest Territory," Biloine Whiting Young wrote in *River of Conflict, River of Dreams*, a seminal biography of the river that spans three hundred years of its development.

Then came the steamboat, the greatest game changer yet for river travel. An inventor named John Fritch built a floating contraption with a series of steam-powered, oarlike paddles in 1786, two decades before partners Robert Livingston and Robert Fulton built their own steamboat in Pittsburgh. Fulton's first boats required more draft than would be available on the Upper Mississippi, though, so it wasn't until Henry M. Shreve (the namesake of Shreveport, Louisiana) built a steamboat on the hull of a keelboat that such craft could be operated on the shallow upper stretch of the river.

"Some Upper Mississippi River steamboats drew as little as 18 inches of water," Young wrote. "Their captains claimed they could sail them on dew, or run them for miles on the suds from a keg of beer."

The earliest steamboats had paddle wheels mounted on each side, but later builders placed a single paddle wheel on the back. The main deck was usually open space reserved for cargo, passengers, and cordwood for fuel. There often was a second deck for passengers and a third, called the texas deck, for the crew, as well as a pilothouse for the captain.

The first steamboat on the Upper Mississippi was the *Virginia* in the spring of 1823. It was 118 feet long and lacked all the grace and grandeur that would be associated with steamboats in years to come. The *Virginia's* makers hoped it would become the first craft to make it from St. Louis to Fort Snelling, so the ship was no bigger than a keelboat and had no cabin or pilothouse. The steam engine sat on the boat's deck, and travelers were protected from the elements by a roofed cargo box. The passengers on the *Virginia's* historic maiden run included a female missionary headed for the lead mine region; an Indian agent returning to Washington, DC; a Kentucky family bound for the mines at Galena; and Great Eagle, a Sauk chief returning from a meeting in St. Louis with General William Clark. Other members of Great Eagle's tribe walked along the shore, easily keeping pace with the slow-moving boat.

At times, it was slower than slow. At Rock Island the boat became hung up for several days in a dangerous stretch of rapids. When it finally got moving, there were frequent stops so passengers and crew members could cut more firewood for fuel. At one point Great Eagle advised the captain which channel to take, but the captain spurned the Sauk leader's advice and got stuck on a sandbar. Great Eagle jumped overboard and made it to the shore, where he joined his people and proceeded on foot.

Finally, the *Virginia* reached Fort Snelling, Young wrote, "belching smoke from her chimneys and exhausting steam from her escape pipes." The sound so startled Indians at the fort that many of them fled into the nearby woods.

The *Virginia* made the seven-hundred-mile trek in twenty days, including the five days it was stuck on sandbars and in the Rock Island rapids. It would make only one more journey before suffering a mishap and sinking, but not before proving its point.

"The ramshackle craft demonstrated that steamboats could navigate the river and its rapids," Young wrote. "With transportation assured, the magnet of the river began to draw commerce and settlers. A door had been opened, and what began as a trickle of people moving north on the river soon turned into a flood."

And the flood rode on steamboats that multiplied as fast as builders could produce them. Between 1830 and 1840, more than 700 steamboats joined the river fleet, and by 1880 more than 4,800 paddle wheels had been built.

The La Crosse Harbor. WHI IMAGE ID 48627

Still, the earliest boats were often crude, dirty, and lacking many comforts. Even when individual staterooms became common, they were small, with poor lighting and sanitation facilities. George Byron Merrick, who grew up as a "levee rat" on the river in Prescott, Wisconsin, and later spent years working on the *Fanny Harris* and other steamboats, wrote in *Old Times on the Upper Mississippi* that deck crews "of the lowest order" also made for uncomfortable conditions.

Members of Merrick's forty-man crew were "picked up alongshore at St. Louis, Galena, Dubuque, and St. Paul from the riffraff of the levee," he wrote. "They would get drunk whenever they could get whiskey; and as the boat carried hundreds of barrels of this liquor each trip, it required eternal vigilance on the part of

A group of adults and children awaits two passenger steamboats along the Mississippi River near Clinton, Iowa. WHI IMAGE ID 71940

the mates and watchmen to prevent the crew from broaching a barrel and getting fighting drunk and mutinous."

Mark Twain had a more nuanced take on early steamboat crews, describing them as "heavy fighters, reckless fellows, every one, elephantinely jolly, foul-witted, profane, prodigal of their money . . . prodigious braggarts, yet, in the main, honest, trustworthy, faithful to promises and duty and often picturesquely magnanimous."

Feeding hundreds of crew members and passengers three times a day on a floating vehicle with only small supplies of fresh food was a difficult feat not always achieved. "It was a saying on the river that if you wished to save on the meals a passenger was entitled to on his trip, you took him through the kitchen the first thing when he came on board," Merrick wrote. "The inference was that after seeing the food in course of preparation he would give it a wide berth when it came on the table."

Still, steamboats made it possible for commerce to prosper, and they carried optimistic settlers by the thousands to new lands and cities. Passage was relatively cheap; as late as 1880, fares were just three cents a mile, including the cost of meals. "It was almost cheaper to ride a steamboat than stay home," author Ron Larson noted in *Upper Mississippi River History*.

After the Civil War, boats grew in size and boasted more amenities, especially as more passengers began traveling for pleasure instead of merely for transportation. The nicest boats featured fine furniture, chandeliers, better china and silver than many people had at home, stained-glass windows, and grand saloons for entertaining passengers, which usually included gambling in its many forms. Exterior construction included jigsaw carpentry in what became known as the steamboat Gothic style. The white, multidecked boats were often likened to wedding cakes. Or, as Twain put it, "Steamboats are like wedding cakes without the complications."

In addition to passengers and freight, steamboats also carried a whiff of an exotic world far beyond the plain little river towns at which they stopped. In *Old Man River*, Paul Schneider includes this recollection from a local newspaper editor: "A steamboat coming from New Orleans brings to the remote villages of our streams and the very doors of the cabins, a little Paris, a section of Broadway, or a slice of Philadelphia . . . with pianos and stocks of novels, and cards, and dice, and flirting and love-making, and drinking, and champagne, and on the deck, perhaps, three hundred fellows who have seen alligators and neither fear whiskey or gunpowder."

No wonder the rustics eagerly awaited arriving boats.

Another change after the war was in the makeup of the roustabouts. Gone were "the riffraff of the levee"; in their place were crews largely consisting of freed slaves, some of whom also played in musical groups common at the time that entertained passengers in the evening. Merrick said these crews "performed the arduous tasks set for them with a blithe and jocund buoyancy of spirits that robbed the labor of much of the horror with which it had been viewed by the passengers" previously.

At least one frequent passenger agreed, a Miss Grace King, who, as described in Merrick's later history of the Diamond Jo line, seemed almost overcome with sensuous vapors in describing her experience:

"And the roustabouts throwing the rope from the perilous end of the dangling gang-plank. And the dangling roustabouts hanging like drops of water from it—dropping sometimes twenty feet to the land—dropping into the river itself to the infinite amusement of his brother rousters. And when the great boat is safely 'made fast,' what a rolling of barrels and shouldering of sacks and singing of Jim Crow songs and pacing of Jim Crow steps."

"This wasn't work," Merrick added. "It was a frolicsome spectacle not all calculated to give the passengers the blues."

The glory days of the steamboat lasted from about 1840 to 1880, when famous boats such as the *Natchez,* the *Robert E. Lee,* and the *J. M. White* plied the river. But as revolutionary as the steamboat had been, other advancements in bridge building and expansion of the railroads eventually reduced its usefulness and numbered its days. Merrick, who left Wisconsin's steamboat business to take part in the Civil War, returned in 1876 to a river he barely recognized.

"I found a half dozen railroads centering in St. Paul, and these were doing the work of the hundred steamboats that I had left running in 1862 . . . and the profession of piloting was at an end."

It was the same for Twain when he returned to tour the river more than twenty years after he romanticized the steamboat era in his seminal work, *Life on the Mississippi*. "When I was a boy," he wrote, "there was but one permanent ambition among my comrades in our village on the west bank of the Mississippi River. That was to be a steamboatman."

No wonder that upon his return he was shocked by what he saw on the levees.

"Half a dozen sound-asleep steamboats where I used to see a solid mile of wide-awake ones! This was melancholy, this was woeful. The absence of the pervading and jocund steamboatman from the billiard saloon was soon explained. He was absent because he is no more. His occupation is gone, his power has passed away, he is absorbed into the common herd . . . Here was desolation indeed.

"Mississippi steamboating was born about 1812; at the end of thirty years it had grown to mighty proportions; and in less than thirty more it was dead. A strangely short life for so majestic a creature."

PLACES OF INTEREST

The *American Queen*, along with the *Queen of the Mississippi* and the recently built *American Eagle*, have about thirty scheduled stops in La Crosse each summer. The dates for those stops are available at www .explorelacrosse.com, but because of frequent delays or changes in schedule, visitors are advised to check with the Chamber of Commerce, 800-658-9424.

The National Mississippi River Museum & Aquarium, 350 E. 3rd St., Dubuque, has an extensive steamboat exhibit that includes the *William M. Black*, a 277-foot vessel permanently moored in the Ice Harbor.

The George M. Verity River Museum, Victory Park, Mississippi River Dr., Keokuk, Iowa, is housed in a retired steamboat and is open daily from April to November. www.geomverity.org

15

The Most Terrible Conflagration

For all the ways they revolutionized travel on the Mississippi and spurred the movement of settlers to western places, the steamboats that added so much romance to the river came with certain unavoidable drawbacks.

They sank, often sent to their watery graves by boiler explosions that left the wooden vessels afire and passengers in flight. Others sank from damage caused by sandbars or other underwater hazards, or aboveground hazards such as bridge piers. Others succumbed to natural elements such as tornados. In *Old Times on the Upper Mississippi*, longtime captain George Byron Merrick said that of the 360 paddle wheels that operated on the upper river between 1823 and 1863, seventy-two were lost in various, and often tragic, mishaps.

Not all disasters were equal. The worst disaster on the Mississippi—perhaps the deadliest in American history—involved the steamer *Sultana*, a side-wheeler carrying some 2,300 soldiers home from the Civil War in 1865. In the darkest of ironies, an estimated 1,700 men who had survived the horrors of the war died en route to their homes when boilers exploded a few miles from Memphis and fire swept through the ship.

Twenty-five years later, the steamer *Sea Wing* was carrying more than two hundred passengers on a pleasure cruise on Lake Pepin when a severe storm struck the ship and an attached barge, killing almost a hundred terrified revelers.

The burning of the *War Eagle* in La Crosse in May 1870 can't match those events in the number of casualties, but in so many ways it stands out from the hundreds of ships that sank on the Mississippi over the years. Just five victims were confirmed dead in the aftermath of the terrible fire that gave the river "the appearance of an immense sea of blood," as the *La Crosse Evening Democrat* described it.

A century and a half later, the disaster still occupies a prominent place in both La Crosse history and current events.

The *War Eagle*, a 296-ton side-wheeler, was one of several vessels that carried the name but was clearly the best known. Built in Fulton, Ohio, in 1854, she was known as one of the finest boats on the Mississippi River, boasting onboard barbershops, washrooms, velvet carpets, and high-end furnishings for passengers. She initially was owned by the Galena Packet Company in Illinois. The same year she was built, the *War Eagle* was one of the most prominent steamboats in the Grand Excursion that marked the connection of railroad service to the Mississippi River.

During the Civil War she carried troops to battle and later was acquired by the La Crosse & St. Paul Packet Company, known as the "White Line" for the white stripe painted on smokestacks. At one point, the *War Eagle* bested the steamer *Tishimingo* in a race, further establishing her place atop the hierarchy of river craft. In an age when the average life of a steamboat was five years or less, the *War Eagle* was in service for sixteen years.

In 1870 the ship was carrying goods and passengers between Galena and St. Paul, with stops at several ports during the

The *War Eagle*. MURPHY LIBRARY SPECIAL COLLECTIONS, UNIVERSITY OF
WISCONSIN-LA CROSSE

forty-four-hour trip. One was at La Crosse, to pick up freight
at the Milwaukee Road Railroad Depot on the Black River, as
well as passengers, including settlers carrying their families and
belongings to the new frontier. While the ship was docked on
the night of May 14, Captain Thomas Cushing noticed a leaking
barrel of kerosene amid the cargo and instructed the ship's cooper,
William T. Bennett, to tighten the bands on the leaking barrel
and several others.

A lantern was the culprit. Bennett later said he took a watch-
man's lantern in his hand and "All of a sudden the lantern was all
ablaze inside and in a moment it burst and the kerosene on the
floor caught. In an instant the flames reached the cabin floor. My
pantaloons caught and two or three standing near said, 'Jump into
the river.' I did so and put myself out."

In hindsight it seems remarkable more lives were not lost.
Thirty to forty passengers were on board when the fire began to
rapidly spread. Some made it into a small boat that was lowered

to the water, while others jumped into the river between the boat and the wharf, including the five who drowned. Meanwhile the fire spread across the dock, engulfing the Milwaukee Road's depot, three freight warehouses, and a freight train whose cars and contents were later valued at more than $250,000.

In the darkness there was terror, confusion over how many had died, and, as one passenger told the *La Crosse Morning Leader*, "a scene to appall the timid and awe the brave. Words are utterly inadequate to describe the terrible scene in the conflagration, the consternation and the dismay."

Another creatively descriptive witness told the *La Crosse Evening Democrat*, "It was one of the most terrible fires that has ever startled the people of the northwest. The sky was cloudless yet the fire was so brilliant that it cast a shadow for miles toward the moon. The Mississippi River presented the appearance of an immense sea of blood. The opposite shore and the island seemed to have clothed themselves in ghostly garments and the trees and shrubbery danced in the changing lights like the imaginary spectre of the graveyard. Dogs, cattle and poultry gave vent to those peculiar cries that indicate distress, showing that even the dumb creatures realized the peril of the hour."

Initial reports put the death toll higher, and many stories written since have used conflicting numbers, but the La Crosse Historical Society puts the official count at five because no more can be confirmed. Of the known victims, the most tragic story was that of Mary Ulrich, the eighteen-year-old niece of a German-language newspaper editor in La Crosse. She was en route to Alma, Wisconsin, to serve as bridesmaid for her sister's wedding and had been placed in the protective custody of Felix Spiller, the boat's black barber who had agreed to watch out for her. As flames approached, Spiller urged the young woman to jump with him into the river. A deckhand later reported the two

Another disaster along the Mississippi involved the sternwheel *J.S.*, shown here, which caught fire on June 25, 1910. Eleven hundred passengers were rescued, and only two people died. The boat's hull lies on the bottom of the Mississippi. WHI IMAGE ID 5929

were "found clasped together, the barber evidently having tried to save the girl but both drowned," wrote La Crosse historian Robert Taunt. Ulrich's body was taken to her uncle's home, where a large gathering of citizens attended her funeral.

Spiller's body was given over to the coroner for burial in a potter's field.

A few artifacts from the *War Eagle* were salvaged in the days after the fire, but for many years the ship lay undisturbed on the floor of the Black River near its meeting with the Mississippi. In later years, before laws were enacted to protect shipwrecks, divers retrieved hundreds of items from the site, ranging from tools to a beam from the ship's hull to a porcelain hand from a doll. One local diver who spent ten summers exploring the wreckage and bringing up artifacts later said in a television interview that he returned just one item to the ship—an old skull.

All these years later it is hard to visit La Crosse and not take note of the event. That small steamship on city street signs? It's the image of the *War Eagle*. The wall-size mural on Second Street? It's the *War Eagle*, again. The La Crosse Historical Society annually commemorates the fire on *War Eagle* Day, and the story continues to find new readers whenever it is retold.

"It's a really good story," said Taunt, "and it should be a Hollywood movie."

As the local historical society's curator once said, "The *War Eagle* is our *Titanic*."

PLACES OF INTEREST

A historical marker reciting the story of the *War Eagle* is in Riverside Park, near 410 E. Veterans Memorial Drive.

Many artifacts from the *War Eagle* are on display at the nearby Riverside Museum, operated by the La Crosse Historical Society. www.lchshistory.org/ riverside-museum

16

The City that Named an Actress

At least one famous American ac-
tress has been named for a community along the Mississippi River.
If the name of this community
originally proposed by its founders
had stuck, Winona Ryder, born not
far away in Olmstead County, Minnesota, might have become Monte-

zuma Ryder instead. Even Johnny Depp might have found that
a little strange.

But the name Montezuma, likely after the famous Aztec em-
peror, was abandoned in the nascent city's earliest days in favor
of Winona, a name derived from the Indian word for firstborn
daughter, *We-no-nah*. The girl born Winona Laura Horowitz, because her parents liked the sound of the nearby city's name, might
have changed her last name when she went Hollywood, but she
carried her link to the Mississippi riverfront with her.

Of course, even Montezuma wasn't the first name for this
community originally platted on a sandbar of the Mississippi.
Long before the city was founded in 1851, Native Americans had
been living here for thousands of years on what was then known
as Wapasha's Prairie, named for a succession of Mdewakanton

The Winona levee, sometime between 1870 and 1880. WHI IMAGE ID 5625

Dakota leaders named Wapasha I, Wapasha II, Wapasha III, and Wapasha IV.

The first white people to arrive here were missionaries, in 1839, though their intentions were not embraced by the Dakota, who harassed the newcomers until they left after just one year. But as other settlers moved in, the Indians ultimately were outnumbered and their population was ravaged by disease. The Indians were forced to cede their land on Wapasha's Prairie through a series of treaties with the US government, including a major treaty signed by Wapasha III in 1851.

"You have requested us to sign these papers and have told these people it is for their benefit," he said in a speech that year. "I do not think so."

Appropriate for a community that would become a major steamboat port, the community now known as Winona was founded by Captain Orrin Smith, a steamboat pilot on the Galena to Fort Snelling route, who knew the land on the western side of the river would be quickly claimed in the wake of the treaty signed by Wapasha III. On October 15, 1851, Smith dropped his ship's carpenter, Erwin Johnson, and two other men on the riverfront to claim it and the surrounding prairie for a town site. Johnson and Smith favored the name Montezuma, but when businessman Henry D. Huff bought an interest in the town site two years later, he persuaded Captain Smith to change the name to Winona.

Growth came rapidly to the new city. Steamboats brought commerce and new residents, and Winona became a frequent stopping place for boats headed up and down the river carrying lumber, wheat, and other goods. By 1860 Winona had nearly 2,500 residents and soon was averaging more than a thousand steamboat arrivals and departures each year.

The earliest new residents were Yankees from New England, followed by a number of German immigrants who quickly established successful businesses. But in the late 1850s Winona witnessed the arrival of another group that would make a lasting imprint on the city's makeup and culture: Kashubian immigrants from Poland's Baltic Coast. In Europe, Kashubians had been ruled over and looked down upon by Germans, Poles, and Swedes, according to Winona's Polish Cultural Institute and Museum. To this day, the city is considered by many to be the Kashubian capital of America.

The Bronk and Eichman families came first, followed by families with such names as Felckowski, Kiedrowski, Kukowski, Libera, Reszke, and Walenski. They wrote to relatives about their new home in America and soon others followed; by 1900, about four thousand of Winona's five thousand Polish residents—in a city of nearly twenty thousand—were Kashubians. Lacking English, the Kashubians initially kept to themselves, taking labor-intensive jobs in mills and on the water, instead of farming as they had in Europe. A Polish-language newspaper edited by

Hieronim Derdowski served these immigrants, who largely kept their Kashubian accents and vocabulary but eventually began to identify with the far more numerous Polish Americans.

Today, Kashubian culture and language are preserved at the Polish Cultural Institute and Museum. Other reminders of the group's presence can be found at the ornate Basilica of St. Stanislaus Kostka, one of only two basilicas in Minnesota, where stained-glass windows dedicated to various saints bear Polish inscriptions. Four thousand people were said to have stood in the rain to watch the cornerstone get placed in 1894, and even more came for the first service one year later. For the community, this was no small accomplishment. While the grand churches of Europe were often funded by the rich and the powerful, in Winona regular parishioners raised $85,000, considered a fortune at the time, to pay for their church. Winona's Polish and Kashubian immigrants wanted to make a statement with their church. "They came from beautiful European structures, and they wanted something that reminded them of home," a priest said during a centennial observance.

The three decades between 1870 and 1900 comprised Winona's golden era, when fortunes were made—and jobs were filled—by wheat milling, lumbering, and transportation over river and rail. Winona's wagon manufacturing business produced thousands of wagons a year and sent them off around the globe. And mills in Winona such as the Northwest Mills Company not only processed wheat for human consumption but also made, as one boosterish pamphlet titled *Winona Beautiful* claimed, "a sugar stock food that cattle cry for like children for Castoria."

Another business brought national notice to little Winona: the personal and home care products produced and promoted by J. R. Watkins, who began his rise to prominence by creating a pain-relieving ointment called Red Liniment for harried housewives. Watkins began working out of his Plainview, Minnesota,

Levee Park. WINONA COUNTY HISTORICAL SOCIETY

home in 1868 and gained prominence by offering America's first
money-back guarantee for unhappy customers. Enough were
happy, though, that Watkins later moved his growing company
to Winona, where he commissioned noted architect George W.
Maher to design a headquarters building boasting a seventy-
foot-high rotunda dome coated in gold leaf, more than two
hundred stained-glass skylights, and three Tiffany stained-glass
windows. (Thus Winona's claim to be America's Stained Glass
Capital.) Today the Watkins company offers some 350 products
and maintains a museum telling the Watkins story.

The same boosterish publication that touted Winona's remarkable cattle feed noted that the city should be credited with
one more title: "the pioneer of river-front parks in America."
Levee Park, created on the waterfront where steamboats once
lined up to load and unload, is "Winona's piece de resistance—
the place to which we take strangers and ask them if they ever
saw anything like it.

"Winona was the first city to transform an unsightly narrow strip of river bank, the catch-all of tins cans and dead cats, into a beauty spot."

Levee Park now sits within sight of the interstate bridge. A stone wall still serves to keep the river in its place, but the park is also a center of entertainment, featuring concerts, community programs, and other uses.

PLACES OF INTEREST

Winona County History Center, 160 Johnson St., Winona, operated by the Winona County Historical Society, features permanent and changing exhibits, along with historical programs. www.winonahistory.org

J. R. Watkins Museum and Store, 150 Liberty St., www.jrwatkins.com

Polish Cultural Institute and Museum, 102 Liberty St., www.polishmuseumwinona.org

Minnesota Marine Art Museum, 800 Riverview Dr., featuring marine and maritime art as well as works by European and American masters. www.mmam.org/

Basilica of St. Stanislaus Kostka, 625 East 4th St., http://ssk-sjn.weconnect.com/

17

Alma,
a Nineteenth-Century River Town

Buena Vista Overlook, the breath-
taking sandstone balcony set five
hundred feet over the little town of
Alma, Wisconsin, is known for river
scenery that stretches miles north
and south, for its eagle-eye views of
eagles and other birds, and for Tech-
nicolor sunsets over the Mississippi.

For good reasons Buena Vista is one of the most aptly named and
popular spots to stop along the Great River Road.

But as much as it is a platform to consider the Alma of now, a
historic community just two streets wide busily engaged in tourism and recreation, Buena Vista Overlook is a perfect place to remember the Alma of then, back when the city was a major player
in Wisconsin's great logging era. It was all thanks to its situation
on the Mississippi River, if not exactly the river you see today.

At its founding as a supply spot for cordwood for steamboat
fuel in 1848, Alma was originally known as Twelve Mile Bluff,
named for a landmark stone feature that steamboat pilots could
make out from the mouth of the Chippewa River, twelve miles to

An elevated view of Alma. WHI IMAGE ID 25899

the north. The name change some years later was inspired by the battle for the Alma River in the Crimean War, and good thing for that because the prominent stone feature pilots relied on broke off the bluff in 1881 and crashed into the town below, destroying property but causing no injuries.

Its first settlers were mostly Swiss, according to *Alma on the Mississippi*, a history published by the Alma Historical Society and written by Barbara Anderson-Sannes. The main industry in the early years was woodcutting, but as more settlers arrived and the community grew, other businesses sprang up. Among the first was a brewery.

In 1861 Alma became the Buffalo County seat, added a courthouse and a newspaper, and claimed a population of 150 residents. After the Civil War, the logging industry exploded in the timber-rich Chippewa Valley. Wealthy investors who owned large forest tracts decided they would realize greater profits if they skipped local mills and transported their logs to mills farther south on the Mississippi River. It was Alma's good fortune that a channel of the Chippewa River that fed into Beef Slough just north of town was deemed a perfect harbor in which to sort the logs and send them off downriver. In 1867 the Beef Slough Manufacturing, Booming, Long Driving and Transportation Company, known by the unwieldy acronym of BSMBLD&T, was formed, in honor of which the local newspaper expanded its name to *Alma Journal and Beef Slough Advocate.*

Unsurprisingly, the decision to bypass mills in Eau Claire and Chippewa Falls was unpopular with those owners, who challenged Beef Slough in court and, on a few occasions, in physical confrontations. They attempted to block the slough with their own log rafts and cut the company's log booms loose, incidents that became known as the Beef Slough War of 1868. As wars go it wasn't much, resulting in a few arrests but no injuries. Eventually the company prevailed; a few years later, with the arrival of lumber giant Frederick Weyerhauser and his Mississippi Logging Company, operations on the Chippewa became part of a major interstate industry. In the 1880s as many as a dozen steamboats a day arrived at Beef Slough to pick up log rafts, making it one of the busiest ports anywhere.

At the peak of the log run, more than six hundred men worked at Beef Slough, living in camps along the river or in town, where a housing shortage forced several families to share single-family homes.

Good times, those were. In 1885, the first railroad train arrived, Anderson-Sannes wrote, "and the jubilant people of Alma hosted a turkey dinner at the Union House." Throughout the 1880s, an average of more than 250 million board feet of lumber passed through Beef Slough and another nearby shipping point each year, topped by 550 million board feet in the peak year of 1889. It was said to be the largest log sorting and rafting works in

Workers at Beef Slough arrange logs for transport. WHI IMAGE ID 25795

Wisconsin and maybe even the world, rivaled by the Tittabawas-
see booming works in Michigan, which might have challenged
that claim. When winter brought a close to the shipping season,
many of the men left camps and went into the woods to cut more
pine that could be shipped the following spring.

Alma, by then a city of nearly 1,500 residents, was on the map
and on the go.

But then the go began to slow and soon would halt entirely.
By 1900, as the rich pinelands played out, log shipments steadily
declined, and by 1905 activity at the slough was over. What remained of BSMBLD&T was dissolved. When fire claimed the last
mill at the slough in 1911, little evidence remained of the hectic
work that had lasted thirty years.

Ten years later, when the last lumber raft on the Mississippi
River passed Alma on its trip downriver, Anderson-Sannes
wrote, "Thus the region's supply of virgin pine, thought to be

inexhaustible only a generation previous, has disappeared forever."

There was no jubilant turkey dinner on that occasion.

Alma did not disappear, but its population shrank as lumber workers moved on. In 1932, work began on Lock and Dam No. 4 as part of the federal effort to harness the wild river for large-carrier shipping. But the changes that aided barge traffic meant boats could no longer reach Alma's river landings, and the flooding that resulted behind the dam covered islands and changed forever the look and environment of the river. Change had come before, most notably the railroad's impact on river traffic, but the dam ended any semblance of Alma as a river port.

Today Alma, its population of 781 in the 2010 census just half of that at its peak, benefits from its location on the river road and is a popular stopping point for tourists. It bills itself still as a nineteenth-century river town (community motto: "Step into

Beef Slough. WHI IMAGE ID 68937

living history"), preserving much of its early look in a National
Historic District established in 1882, covering nearly 350 acres
and including more than 200 buildings.

Other vestiges of Alma then can be found in the historic photographs of Gerhard Gesell, a German immigrant who for more
than thirty years as a photo artist captured community life and
people in portraits, landscapes, and stereographs. His large-scale
composite of more than 150 early Alma area settlers, "Pioneers
of Buffalo Co., Wis.," was later purchased by Buffalo County and
installed in the courthouse.

Another Gesell, Gerhard and Christine's son Arnold, might
well be Alma's most famous son. After earning a bachelor's degree

from the University of Wisconsin in 1906 and a PhD from Clark University, Arnold Gesell served as an assistant professor at Yale, where in 1915 he earned an MD and established a clinic for the study of child development and psychology. Eventually he became one of America's leading authorities on child rearing and development.

The glory days of Beef Slough, when Alma was a player on the river, might easily elude modern visitors more interested in a glimpse of an eagle or a sunset from Buena Vista Park. But even if washed from sight by time and the tamed Mississippi, those hardworking sawdust days deserve to be remembered.

An example of Gerhard Gesell's iconic Mississippi River photography; here, a group of boys splashes in the river, and the town of Alma can be seen in the distance. WHI IMAGE ID 2083

PLACES OF INTEREST

Alma Area Museum, in the Buffalo County Training School, 505 S. 2nd Street, Alma, has exhibits on Beef Slough and other local history. Open late May to early October, Saturdays and Sundays from 1 to 4 p.m. A slide show of Gerhard Gesell's photographs of early Alma can be viewed at www.almahistory.org/photographyofgesell.html.

Buena Vista Overlook can be reached by a hiking trail from downtown. Or drive County E from downtown to Buena Vista Park and walk to the overlook.

Wings over Alma Nature and Art Center, 118 N. Main St., offers educational and environmental programs and exhibits on birding and other wildlife and features the work of local artists.

18

The Father of Waterskiing

The young man credited with inventing the sport of waterskiing had witnesses to his historic moment on the waters of Lake Pepin in 1922, though at least a few less than honorable observers were rooting more for painful failure than noteworthy achievement.

"We were out there," one witness told a reporter years later, "to see him drown or break his neck."

Ralph Samuelson knew that—he'd heard the jibes and laughter—but he was undeterred. Fortunately for fans of happier history, Samuelson neither died nor drowned, though for a few days in late June of that year, he suffered his share of face plants and painful frustration. Then, on July 2, he shouted "Hit it" to his brother Ben, who sat at the wheel of their small motorboat, raised the tips of his skis out of the water—why hadn't he thought to try that before?—and labored to his feet.

Finally, Ralph Samuelson was skiing on water. The next day he turned nineteen.

While some in his hometown of Lake City, Minnesota, considered Lake Pepin as treacherous, thanks in part to a deadly boat

Lake Pepin. WHI IMAGE ID 122623

disaster from decades before, Samuelson grew up a water rat, fishing, swimming, and clamming in its waters. As a boy, Samuelson had ridden a board pulled by an aquaplane, but that wasn't the same as waterskiing behind a boat.

His first efforts, using barrel staves as skis, left him soaked in failure; he met the same wet end when he tried snow skis on the lake. Finally, he went to the Lake City hardware store and for one dollar each bought two boards eight feet long and nine inches wide. He boiled the tips for three hours, applied clamps and braces to curve them upward, and let them set for two days. He painted the boards to help preserve them, used leather scraps and wood screws to fashion rough bindings, bought one hundred feet of sash cord, and had a blacksmith form an iron ring for a handle.

Actually skiing with the skis would be a bigger challenge than building them. He tried jumping off his brother's boat but couldn't land on his feet. He tried starting with his skis underwater, which launched him face-first every time, to the delight of those watching from shore. Only after deciding to lean back and keep his curved tips above the water did he achieve his dream of gliding on wood over water.

It was, *Waterski* magazine reported decades later in an article titled "The Good Father," "a miraculous birth in the world of sport. A futuristic achievement in a tiny upper Midwest town. And the townsfolk responded with a collective yawn."

"In fact," Samuelson said in his own memoirs, "nothing happened at all." If the Wright brothers became world famous for inventing flight, Ralph and Ben Samuelson were pretty much ignored for their own recreational invention.

That didn't stop Ralph from enjoying the new sport, though. He began doing exhibitions locally and later took his skis and skills on tours through the Midwest, in the process becoming the first man to slalom on skis as well as the first to ski jump. Again, not without a few stumbles. His first attempt to ski off a ramp

A group watches an aquaplane pulling a skier on Lake Pepin.
LAKE CITY HISTORICAL SOCIETY

An older Samuelson, holding a set of monogrammed skis.

failed when his skis stuck to the incline, but after he applied a layer of lard to grease the way, he succeeded. In 1925 he skied behind a World War I Curtiss Flying Boat at eighty miles per hour, thus becoming the first speed skier.

Samuelson's skiing career ended in 1937 when, while helping to build a boat livery in Florida, he broke his back in a construction accident. He later moved to Pine Island, Minnesota, to raise turkeys, where it seemed history—and the sport of waterskiing—forgot about him.

For many years waterskiing enthusiasts engaged in debate over who had created their sport. A Frenchman who had water-skied on the Riviera got some support, while others credited a New York man named Fred Waller, who had water-skied in 1925 in Huntington, New York, after obtaining a patent for what he called "Akwa Skees." In 1963, though, a St. Paul newspaper reporter named Margaret Crimmins found Samuelson's skis in Lake City and ignited new debate over the sport's origin story.

Crimmins made the case for Lake City, especially after photos from as early as 1923 were produced that showed Ralph on his skis.

"The plush and wealthy French Riviera has a paternity suit on its hands, unofficially filed by this scenic little southeastern Minnesota town," she wrote in 1965.

City officials joined the cause, writing to the American Water Ski Association with affidavits in support of Samuelson. In 1966 the association officially agreed, announcing on its magazine cover "Water Skiing Has a New 'Real Father,'" and declaring Lake City as the birthplace of waterskiing, and Ralph Samuelson its inventor. In 1972, on the fiftieth anniversary of his first successful ski, Samuelson was honored by Lake City at its inaugural Water Ski Days festival. In 1977 he attended the groundbreaking of the American Water Ski Hall of Fame in Winter Haven, Florida, where he had been made inductee number one.

Samuelson died of cancer a short time later. In his last years, he enjoyed teaching kids how to ski on Lake Pepin, where a large historical plaque and sculpted wave on the shore now remember his contribution to watery enjoyment.

"Did I feel like a pioneer, like Jesus walking on water?" Samuelson said in an interview years after his first ski. "All I felt was that at long last I had proved to my family, to myself and a lot of fellows who had been laughing at me for months that I could do what I had set out to do."

PLACES OF INTEREST

Lake City celebrates Water Ski Days, featuring waterskiing exhibitions, music in the beer garden, street carnival, and parade, each year on the last full weekend of June.

Samuelson's skis are on display at Lake City Marina, 201 S. Franklin St., Lake City, Minnesota. www .ci.lake-city.mn.us

Pearl of the Lake, a replica 1800s paddleboat, offers cruises on Lake Pepin. www.pearlofthelake.com

19

And the River Runs Unruly

Despite the best human efforts to contain and control the river's water level with dikes, levees, dams, and countless other tax-funded feats of US Army Corps engineering, the Mississippi has a mind of its own. Some years the river's water level falls, creating a navigational nui-

sance. Some years it rises, leaving the contour of its banks a mere suggestion as it creeps into fields and city streets.

And every so often the river rises in such an unruly manner that it sets off a desperate, clock-ticking, man-against-nature cage match, all too often in which nature's unleashed power far exceeds man's ability to push back.

Floods have been a fact of life along the river since before people made their homes on its banks, and the list of notable flood years runs into the dozens. Still, some floods stand out for the drama and destruction, the tragedy and sometimes triumphs that resulted. The Mississippi River flood of 1927, commonly known as the Great Flood of 1927, remains one of the most destructive natural events in American history.

Flood damage. WHI IMAGE ID 66184

In the early months of 1927, heavy rains caused the Mississippi River to swell. In April of that year, a levee in Illinois gave way, quickly followed by others up and down the river, and the river surged beyond its banks. Floodwater covered more than twenty-three thousand square miles of land; at Vicksburg the river was eighty miles wide. Hundreds of thousands of people were displaced, and as many as 250 people died.

The relief efforts that followed disproportionately prioritized white residents over African Americans, even as many black residents of flooded areas were without food, water, or other necessities. In some places, black flood victims were held in camps under the watch of armed guards, and the flood's aftermath scarred race relations as much as high water did the land and cities that it overran. In his 1997 book *Rising Tide: The Great Mississippi Flood of 1927 and How It Changed America,* John M. Barry argued that the mistreatment of black flood victims led to increased northern migration and paved the way for Herbert Hoover's presidency thanks to his role in supervising flood relief.

The Great Flood of 1927 inspired new government programs to ensure the river would not run wild again, but of course it did, and often.

Along the Upper Mississippi, all other floods are measured against the flood of 1965. Conditions that year were such that the flooding was easy to predict, though its severity would still surprise. Heavy snowfall early in the year remained on the ground through a colder than usual March, and rivers and lakes were locked in thick ice. Frost in the ground was deep, so that when temperatures finally began to warm and snow began to melt, the ground could not absorb the water.

"A swift thaw will cause trouble," the *La Crosse Tribune* reported early that April, "and a combination of warm temperatures and rain the next several days could raise havoc, river observers agree."

Right on cue, it began to rain.

"A continent conspired against river dwellers that year," Marc Hequet wrote in a retrospective story for *Big River* magazine years later. "Only one thing is worse than wrestling with a berserk river: wrestling with a freezing cold, ice-chocked berserk river."

Destructive flooding began on northern stretches of the river first, warning cities downriver that they would soon be in for the fight of their lives. Where the Mississippi and Minnesota Rivers merged near St. Paul, many buildings and hundreds of homes were soon standing in water as tall as a man. People began to evacuate, and not just from areas immediately adjacent to the raging river's banks. At Mankato, inland from the Mississippi but where the Minnesota River had already spilled over its banks, more than a quarter of the city's twenty-five thousand residents left their homes.

Throughout the sodden month of April residents up and down the river fought back, of course. High school students were excused from classes to fill sandbags; prisoners were released to lend their labor (in La Crosse, the sheriff's wife employed jail prisoners in her assembly-line sandwich operation, explaining, "I don't want any other women in my kitchen"); and volunteers from communities not threatened by water came to lend a hand in building dikes, watching for leaks in the levees and other tasks. As the river reached and then exceeded flood stage, the National Guard arrived to help with more evacuations.

Some highways buckled, and many others were impassable because they were under water. Ice jammed river channels, further spreading floodwater and threatening bridges, power plants, and natural gas lines. At Mankato, two men whose boat was swamped by floodwater were rescued in daring fashion by a motorist who saw them struggling, pulled the boat off his car rack and motor from his trunk, and risked his own safety to bring them to shore.

At one point President Lyndon Johnson came to inspect the damage and suffering. When one man told him, "Everything is wiped out," all Johnson could answer was "I'm sorry."

Later, looking at more damaged areas, he was heard to mutter, "Horrible, horrible."

For some who had lived all their lives along the river, it was an all too familiar battle. One man who had raised his house two feet after a flood in 1952 discovered he had not raised it nearly enough, though his wife, then seventy-four, told the people who had helped them evacuate, "I'm a river rat. Of course I wasn't afraid."

Some cities were damaged more than others. In Prairie du Chien, the entire fourth ward was under water and, a newspaper reported, "The 24-foot river gauge at the radio station was under water and out of sight." The water was so high that some garages were beginning to float and only the roofs of some houses were above water.

The fight to save Winona, built on a sandbar and thus especially vulnerable, was beyond desperate. Workers at Fountain City struggled to reinforce the spillway on Lock and Dam No. 5A, knowing that if the water broke through, Winona and its residents would be underwater. Winonans did all they could to protect their city in what became known as Operation Eagle.

Colleges closed so students could join the struggle, which eventually involved more than six thousand people. More than one thousand residents of the lowest areas in town were evacuated, and still the water continued to rise. On Easter weekend, though, in mid-April, residents were shocked to learn the water level had dropped eight inches. A portion of railroad line that was part of the dike system across the Mississippi at Bluff Siding, Wisconsin, had given way, releasing floodwater on that side.

An act of God, grateful Winona residents said. But such a convenient reprieve sparked speculation and lasting conspiracy theories that someone lacking God's omnipotence had used dynamite

Flooded railroad tracks in Fountain City. WHI IMAGE ID 24953

Fountain City, ca. 1925. WHI IMAGE ID 31251

on the track in order to boost Winona's chances of survival. Even on the fiftieth anniversary of the flood in 2015, a Winona resident who had fought the flood as a twenty-one-year-old college student called such thinking "a tall tale," but one that refused to die.

"Did somebody blow up the tracks to save Winona?" he told the *Winona Post*. "It's a great old wives tale."

Finally, floodwaters began to recede, in part because high water had moved downriver to threaten communities to the south. Over a period of a month, more than five hundred miles of river from St. Paul to St. Louis experienced flooding, and during that same time at least fourteen people died and thirty-five thousand were forced from their homes. By the end of April the river had largely returned to its banks and residents in northern communities were returning to their homes, where the cleanup was only beginning.

It was a sad task that some riverside residents knew all too well. A reporter asked one woman what it was like to return to a flood-ravaged property.

"The first thing you do," she said, "is cry."

20

Winona and the Maiden's Rock

The story of a heartbroken lover has inspired among writers more than a little alliteration. The saga of the woebegone young Indian woman Winona, who threw herself from one of the prettiest and most romantic spots along the Mississippi River rather than marry a man she didn't  want, is often called a sad story, a tragic tale—even, in one telling, "the Lachrymose Legend of Lover's Leap."

It's all of that, and an old story as well. Zebulon Pike wrote in his journal of learning the tale while exploring the river in 1805, calling it "a wonderful display of sentiment in a savage." In *Life on the Mississippi*, Mark Twain recounted hearing a version (there are many) of "perhaps the most celebrated, as well as the most pathetic, of all the legends of the Mississippi."

It happened, or so pathetic legend has it, on the famously picturesque bluff known as Maiden Rock, near a small community of the same name on Lake Pepin in Wisconsin's Pierce County. Lake Pepin is a broadening of the river, some twenty miles long and up to two miles wide, flanked by dramatic bluff formations that rise hundreds of feet over the water.

Two women pose in front of the statue of Winona, erected in the city of
Winona's Central Park in 1902. WINONA COUNTY HISTORICAL SOCIETY

Winona (sometimes spelled Wenona or Whe-no-nah and an
Indian word for the firstborn daughter) was a member of the
Dakota tribe and the daughter of Chief Red Wing. Winona's
main task was to make beautiful moccasins for her father, by
one account decorated with the wings of red birds that gave her
father his name. Accounts differ on details but most agree that
Winona was in love with a man named White Eagle, a member
of the Ojibwe tribe and thus one of the Dakota's longtime enemies, while her parents and brothers decided she should marry a
Dakota warrior of their choosing.

An early writer on Native American life, Mary Henderson
Eastman, describing in 1849 the story she claimed to have heard
from an old Dakota medicine woman, wrote that Winona refused
to abide by her parents' wishes.

"I do not love him, I will not marry him," was her constant
reply, though she knew that marrying White Eagle instead would
cost him his life. Even as her arranged suitor brought the family
gifts of food and goods to take on an upcoming hunt, Winona
refused to embrace the marriage her parents demanded. As the

party moved downriver, hunters in their canoes suddenly heard a loud shriek from Winona's mother, who was looking up at the bluff from her own canoe.

"Do you not see my daughter?" she said, in Eastman's version. "She is standing close to the edge of the rock."

"She was indeed there," Eastman wrote, "loudly and wildly singing her dirge, an invocation to the Spirit of the Rock, calm and unconcerned in her dangerous position, while all was terror and excitement among her friends below her."

Her family pleaded with her to come down, but as she had refused their other request so did she remain adamant at the top—but only long enough for a final speech.

"You have forced me to leave you. I was always a good daughter, and never disobeyed you; and could I have married the man I love I should have been happy and would never have left you. But you have been cruel to me; you have turned my beloved from the wigwam; you would have forced me to marry a man I hated. I go to the house of spirits."

And before their horrified eyes, she threw herself from the rock.

Some tellings of the tragic tale say Winona threw herself into the water, which any tourist on the Great River Road could see would have been unlikely given the rock's distance from the river, while others say she died on the rocks below. In one fantastic version included in *Echoes of Our Past*, a collection of historical anecdotes by writer Myer Katz of La Crosse, one of Red Wing's men struck Winona's beloved with an arrow as they fled from the village and he fell dead in her arms. If true it would make Winona not only a great leaper but a very strong woman as well, because "Holding her lover in her arms the beautiful Winona hurled herself and her dead love White Eagle from the bluffs and fell with him into the deep waters of the Mississippi, their love unrequited and unfulfilled."

An engraving of Maiden's Rock. WHI IMAGE ID 95897

Other accounts have a less romantic ending. In *A Treasury of Mississippi River Folklore* by B. A. Botkin, the story ends with her death, as others did, but adds, "As to Winona's warrior, it is said that he lived for many years a hermit, and finally died a madman. So runneth many a song of life."

And then there was the legend told to Twain, which differed in a most significant way. That telling, by "an old gentleman" who had joined Twain's boat ride up the river, agreed in large part with most other accounts until the fateful day of her unwanted wedding when Winona ran to the rock "and, standing on its edge, upbraided her parents who were below, for their cruelty, and then, singing a death-dirge, threw herself from the precipice and dashed them in pieces on the rock below."

"Dashed who in pieces—her parents?" Twain asked.

"Yes."

"There are fifty Lover's Leaps along the Mississippi from whose summit disappointed Indian girls have jumped," said Twain, "but this is the only jump in the lot that turned out in the right and satisfactory way. What became of Winona?"

Happy ever after, the old gentleman explained. "She was a good deal jarred up and jolted; but she got herself together before the coroner reached the fatal spot; and 'tis said she sought and married her true love, and wandered with him to some distant clime, where she lived happy ever after, her gentle spirit mellowed and chastened by the romantic incident."

Of course, the more tragic telling of Winona's leap had more cachet—and more staying power. In 2002, Emilio DeGrazia of Winona, Minnesota, the city most linked to the legend, wrote and produced a popular play titled *Winona: A Romantic Tragedy*. And back in the 1920s, a Minneapolis lyricist and a New York composer collaborated for years on an opera based on the legend that was given a hearing at the Metropolitan Opera House in New York at the urging of President Harding. The opera included not only the story of Winona but also other Indian legends and traditions that, as Twain noted, were commonplace.

One is associated with the Falls of St. Anthony in the Twin Cities, where an Ojibwe woman, also the daughter of a chief, had been cruelly treated by her warrior husband. "Goaded to the quick by repeated wrongs, she finally resolved to release herself from every trouble, and her child from evil friends, by departing for the Spirit Land, and the Falls were to be the gateway to that promised heaven," read the account in *A Treasury of Mississippi River Folklore*. Paddling toward the falls, "She sang a wild death song—for a moment her canoe trembled on the brow of the watery precipice, and in an instant more the mother and child were forever lost in the foam below."

One more soap opera saga gave name to Virgin Island, a small island in the Mississippi River a few miles south of St. Paul. In this Dakota legend, when the warrior beloved by Chief Little Crow's daughter was killed by Ojibwe warriors a few days before their planned wedding, she was so overcome by grief that she threw herself in the water and swam to the island. When she did not return a search party followed, only to find she had hanged herself. And while the name carries a certain presumption, the spot was forever after called Virgin Island.

PLACES OF INTEREST

Maiden Rock, the bluff, is just south of the community of Maiden Rock on Highway 35.

21

Red Wing, the Shoe Leather City

In the 1800s the most eagerly an-
ticipated day in a Mississippi River
town, and especially on the upper
stretch where long winters iced the
waters and chilled community life,
was the first spring day when the
river once again ran free. In his 1933
history of early Red Wing, C. A. Ras-
mussen described the tension of the winter-weary citizenry of
this Minnesota river town as the long-awaited day approached:

> Long before the ice had gone out on Lake Pepin, which
> was the obstacle, throngs assembled at the various corners
> around town and made wagers on the time of the opening,
> discussed the possibilities from every angle and looked for-
> ward with keenest anticipation to the day when they might
> once again deal with the outside world with comfort and
> ease for those times.

The view from street corners was limited, though, so the most
impatient citizens scaled the landmark formation known as Barn
Bluff, hoping for the first glimpse of a steamboat coming upriver.

But if the wait was excruciating, the payoff lit the cannon of exaltation.

"Then would come the welcome news that a boat was in sight; the event would be heralded by the ringing of bells and the population would gather on the levee almost to a man to welcome the landing," Rasmussen wrote. "It was the signal of new life in the community, a resurrection from the dormant stage which had prevailed through winter. It was the happiest day of the year."

Red Wing, Minnesota, has long drawn both life and livelihoods from the Mississippi River. Indians lived in this river valley long before the first white man, explorer and Franciscan priest Father Louis Hennepin, arrived in April 1680. In 1805, Colonel Zebulon Pike spent time at the site of today's city during his exploration of the Upper Mississippi, and in 1823—the same year the first steamboat, the *Virginia*, passed by on its way to Fort Snelling—army officer Major Long suggested Red Wing as the moniker for the emerging settlement, named for a series of tribal leaders who used a swan's wing dyed in red as their emblem.

The land on the western side of the Mississippi was not open for settlement by white people until the Dakota signed away their land rights in the 1851 Treaty of Mendota. Red Wing was platted in 1853, but well before that a few settlers—especially missionaries and their families intent on converting Indians to Christianity—had managed to move in. The resident Dakotas resisted both conversion and the white intruders for several decades but eventually superior numbers prevailed, hostilities ended, treaties were reached, and the Dakota people were removed from Minnesota in the 1860s.

Red Wing quickly became a popular destination for new settlers, many from the eastern United States but also immigrants from Switzerland, Germany, and other places. Home to just 1,251 people in 1860, Red Wing grew to a community of more than

The Red Wing waterfront. WHI IMAGE ID 73678

four thousand residents ten years later, primarily because of the wheat trade. Large warehouses were built along the river to hold wheat for shipping, and by the early 1870s Red Wing was one of the most important wheat-trading centers in the world, shipping several million bushels of wheat on river barges every year.

Downtown Red Wing. WHI IMAGE ID 85643

Arrival of the railroads diminished the city's wheat shipments by water, but by then the community had diversified enough with other industries to not only survive but to prosper. For many years the limestone bluffs that tower along the river made Red Wing a hub for making and quarrying lime, and in 1877 the Red Wing Stoneware Company began producing stoneware and pottery that spread the city's name far and wide. Other potters followed, turning the plentiful local clay into popular consumer products, activities that continue today.

In 1905, a Red Wing shoe merchant named Charles Beckman was unhappy with the quality of boots available for his customers, and he decided to make his own instead. With partners, Beckman founded the Red Wing Shoe Company, and before long their workers were producing more than one hundred pairs of shoes a day. Just as pottery had made the name of Red Wing more recognizable, Red Wing shoes and boots were soon a national brand. When the company celebrated its one-hundredth anniversary in 2005, some sixty employees and retirees combined their efforts to built the World's Largest Boot—20 feet long, 16 feet high, weighing 2,300 pounds and lacking only a customer 120 feet tall to try it on. It stands today in the company's flagship store on Main Street, a monument to countless Red Wing shoemakers through the years.

Like all communities, though, Red Wing was not immune to tragedy. And as fate would have it, the very river that brought a city the happiest day of its year also caused the darkest day in its history, an event known forever as the *Sea Wing* disaster.

It began as a Sunday lark. On July 13, 1890, more than 215 excursionists had packed the stern-wheeled steamer *Sea Wing* on a cruise to a summer encampment of the Minnesota National Guard's First Regiment at Camp Lakeview on Lake Pepin. It was a hot, humid day and signs of an impending storm were impossible to ignore, but after one rain had passed, captain and co-owner David Niles Wethern decided to board the passengers on the *Sea Wing* and an attached barge for the return trip. Five miles out on Lake Pepin en route to Red Wing, however, straight-line winds and a raging thunderstorm hit and capsized the doomed vessel, throwing many passengers into the water and drowning many more who were trapped inside.

The barge stayed afloat and eventually drifted aground, sparing its passengers, but nearly a hundred lives were lost. By daybreak forty-two bodies had been recovered, and thirty-two more were found the next day. The dramatic, desperate search for victims—searchers even dynamited the lake in a futile effort to raise bodies to the surface—was fodder for macabre headlines in Twin Cities newspapers. "The Tornado on Pepin's Treacherous Bosom the Crowning Calamity of all Minnesota Annals," one headline blared, while another called Red Wing "City of the Dead."

And it was.

"Red Wing was virtually paralyzed by the disaster," according to an exhibit in the Goodhue County Historical Society, the oldest county historical society in Minnesota. "Of the dead, 77 were from the city and surrounding townships. Church bells tolled incessantly as funeral processions traversed the streets for four days. There were 44 burials on Tuesday alone."

Of fifty-seven women and girls on board, only seven survived. Couples engaged to be married died together, a mother drowned with her baby in her arms, two sisters were grabbed by their hair by would-be rescuers but died when their saviors lost their grip. Fred J. Christ, one of three saloonkeepers who died, is said to have one of the most impressive monuments in Red Wing's Oakwood Cemetery.

Captain Wethern survived to face considerable criticism that was only slightly tempered by the reality that he had lost his wife and youngest son in the tragedy. Eventually federal steamboat inspectors found Wethern guilty of "unskillfullness" and overloading the boat and suspended his license. Apparently not superstitious, however, Wethern later refloated the hull of the *Sea Wing* and again used it on the Mississippi.

Today Red Wing places strong emphasis on historic preservation. One of the most prominent buildings among many nicely preserved downtown structures is the elegant St. James Hotel, established in 1875 in the glory days of the wheat trade. It became so known for its dining and hospitality that the railroad that passed on tracks between the hotel and the river changed its schedule so passengers could disembark and dine at the St. James. Now grandly restored and owned by the Red Wing Shoe Company, still the city's largest employer, the hotel also houses the American Ski Jumping Hall of Fame and Museum, honoring Red Wing's claim as the birthplace of ski jumping in America.

PLACES OF INTEREST

Goodhue County Historical Society, 1166 Oak St., Red Wing, has exhibits on Native American history, immigration, river exhibits and more. www.goodhue countyhistory.org

Pottery Museum of Red Wing, 240 Harrison St., www .potterymuseumredwing.org

Red Wing Shoe Store & Museum, 315 Main St., www .redwing.redwingshoestore.com

Red Wing Marine Museum, 935 Levee Rd., houses a large collection of Red Wing Thorobred Marine Engines along with artifacts and photographs of local river history. www.redwingmarinemuseum.com

American Ski Jumping Museum and Hall of Fame, 406 Main St. in the mezzanine level of the St. James Hotel, www.americanskijumping.com

Barn Bluff hiking trails range from difficult to moderate/easy. Maps are available at the visitor center in the historic train depot at 418 Levee St. on the riverfront, which also houses the Red Wing Arts Association, www.redwingartsassociation.org. Historic walking tour maps are also available at the visitor center.

22

Fort Snelling, Outpost on the River

Colonel Zebulon Pike arrived in the upper Midwest in 1805 with orders from the US Army to establish better relations with the Dakota Indians, locate the headwaters of the Mississippi, and find suitable places for potential military posts. On the first count his impact was minimal, and the spot he declared as the headwaters was not that at all.

But Pike did recommend a dandy spot for a fort near where the Mississippi met the St. Peters (now Minnesota) River. Impressed with the site's advantageous location at the junction of two important river highways, he met with Dakota chiefs on an island that is now part of Fort Snelling State Park and negotiated a pact that allowed the US government to purchase about nine square miles of land for a few hundred dollars' worth of trade goods and a quantity of liquor. Pike left blank the line that should have included a cash purchase price because he had no authority to spend government money, and it wasn't until some years later that Congress authorized a $2,000 payment to complete the treaty.

A pencil drawing of Fort Snelling, created in 1852. WHI IMAGE ID 81527

As Pike himself noted in a report to his commanding officer, General James Wilkinson, "You will please to observe, General, that we have obtained about 100,000 acres for a song."

Not bad for a purchase he valued in his journal at $200,000.

Stand at that site today, outside Historic Fort Snelling that was later built on the land Pike won for relative peanuts, and you will recognize the favorable position on the river that Pike saw, but you won't find the wilderness that surrounded it then. Instead, noisy highways surround the fort and the high-rise buildings of Minneapolis and St. Paul crowd the skyline. As Manhattan was bought for beads, the site of the future Twin Cities was sold for a song.

The Indians had not only been taken, but they were confused at what had been done. Only two of the seven chiefs who had met with Pike signed the treaty, and when Colonel Henry Leavenworth and a troop of soldiers finally arrived in 1819 to build a fort, they found that the Indians had not understood that in accepting Pike's gifts they were agreeing to cede their homelands.

Nonetheless, Leavenworth and his men established a post on the south bank of the Minnesota River. Then, after several soldiers died of scurvy that first winter, the US government abandoned that fort for another of stone construction on the opposite bank. The facility was initially called Fort St. Anthony but was later changed to Fort Snelling to honor the work of Colonel Josiah Snelling, a veteran of the War of 1812 who had taken over from Leavenworth and served as commander for seven years, enlarging and improving barracks and fortifications and doing it all with some frontier style.

"He was a brusque, convivial man, improvident, generous, a lover of good horses and good whisky," Walter Havighurst wrote in *Upper Mississippi: A Wilderness Saga*. "Col. Snelling had a gentleman's taste. Though the post was hundreds of miles from civilization the wives made it a place of social life and ceremony."

In its early years the fort's mission was to oversee the fur trade in the Mississippi Valley, seek peace between oft-warring Indian tribes, and protect the region against British incursion from Canada. But its strategic position as the nation's western-most military installation gave it heightened visibility, and Fort Snelling became something of a destination for travelers. After the steamboat *Virginia* made its first journey to the fort in 1823, other boats followed, bringing merchants, army officers, pioneer settlers, and tourists.

One was the famous artist George Catlin, whose hundreds of images of Indians and frontier landscapes drew even more attention to the area. Catlin outlined a "fashionable tour" that went up the Mississippi from St. Louis to the Falls of St. Anthony near the fort, then back to Prairie du Chien, across the state of Wisconsin to Green Bay and on to Mackinac, Detroit, and other sites. Thousands took the tour, including many from as far away as Europe, and all took in the site of handsome Fort Snelling, ever on duty on the banks of the Mississippi.

"Even then, with its castellated tower crowning the precipitous height above the rivers, Fort Snelling had the air of a storied place," Havighurst wrote.

It was undeniably that, but not all of the stories were happy ones. In the 1820s, slavery was a shameful reality in the Northwest Territory. Josiah Snelling and other officers used slaves as cooks and servants, including a married couple named Dred and Harriet Scott, who were owned by the fort's medical officer, Dr. John Emerson. The Scotts' long legal battle to win freedom from enslavement in what was then a free territory helped to fire the bitter debate in the buildup to the Civil War. Dred Scott had been brought by Emerson to Fort Snelling, where he met and married Harriet, an enslaved woman owned by Indian agent Lawrence Taliaferro. After four years at the fort, Dred and Harriet moved to St. Louis, where in 1846 they sued Dr. Emerson's widow for their freedom, arguing that slavery should not be allowed in free territory at Fort Snelling and other places.

The legal battle lasted for years in multiple state and federal court settings before the US Supreme Court in 1857 ruled 7 to 2 that the Scotts should remain slaves because they were property that could be taken anywhere, even to free territories, by their owners. Southern slave owners were jubilant, but the decision outraged abolitionists and antislavery forces.

Fort Snelling remained in service until 1858, when Minnesota became a state. Western expansion had led to other forts being established in new settlement areas, and Fort Snelling was no longer viewed as necessary, so the fort was closed. The property was sold to a local dreamer who hoped to sell lots and establish a new city known as Fort Snelling, and the parade ground on which soldiers had so long trained became a pasture for sheep.

However, when the Civil War began a few years later, Fort Snelling was ordered reopened as a rendezvous and training center for new soldiers. More barracks were built to handle ever larger units, and between 1861 and 1865 more than twenty-five thousand men passed though Fort Snelling on their way to war. After peace returned, the fort was used as a mustering-out center as well.

In 1862 another war left a tragic incident on Fort Snelling's timeline. It is sometimes called the Dakota War of 1862, the Dakota Conflict, or the Dakota Uprising. Dakota Indians, who had tired of broken treaties, failed promises of food and supplies, and other incidents of mistreatment by the white government, rose up in protest. War broke out, and over a period of weeks bands of warriors attacked settlements throughout the Minnesota territory. As many as six hundred civilians and US soldiers died in the fighting, along with an unknown number of Indians, before troops led by Colonel Henry H. Sibley and trained at Fort Snelling put an end to hostilities.

A military commission led by Sibley investigated Indian killings or assaults on civilians and eventually convicted and sentenced to death 303 Dakota men. However, President Abraham Lincoln later gave a reprieve to all but 39 men, declaring the rest prisoners of war. In the winter of 1862–63, nearly 1,600 Dakota people who had surrendered after the fighting were housed in an internment camp near the fort, where they suffered assaults and beatings by guards and local civilians in addition to unmet hunger and thirst, malnutrition, and disease.

"Amid all the sickness and these great tribulations," a mixed-blood prisoner named Tiwakan, or Gabriel Renville, later recalled, "it seemed doubtful at night whether a person would be alive in the morning."

For a few, death was more deliberate. In autumn of 1865 two of the Dakota leaders—Sakpedan, or Little Six, and Wakanozhanzhan, or Medicine Bottle—were brought to Fort Snelling to be hanged for their part in the war. Wakanozhanzhan, in Havighurst's telling, was "a coarse, ugly fellow who defiantly showed to visitors his arm tattooed with symbols indicating the men, women and children he had scalped—fully 50 in all."

Sakpedan, on the other hand, retained his dignity in the face of death. As his hanging neared, as the story goes, Sakpedan heard a train whistle in the distance and remarked, "As the white man comes in, the Indian goes out."

Fort Snelling continued to serve as a training post in other conflicts, including the Spanish-American War, the war in the Philippines, and World War I. During World War II the fort hosted the Military Intelligence Service Language School, where Japanese Americans were trained to be translators and intelligence workers for the US military. After the war the fort was decommissioned, but its chapel is still in use today, hosting nondenominational services reflecting the site's military past. Historical flags are on display, and the baptismal font was carved from the original tombstone of Elizabeth Snelling, daughter of Colonel Josiah Snelling.

Today Fort Snelling is a National Historic Landmark operated by the Minnesota Historical Society to educate visitors on the fort's military role, the fur trade, the 1862 Dakota War, and slavery in Minnesota. The fort's barracks, store, and hospital are open to visitors, and costumed interpreters are used to personalize the stories of the fort's early days.

PLACES OF INTEREST

Historic Fort Snelling, 200 Tower Ave. in St. Paul, www.historicfortsnelling.org

Nearby are also Fort Snelling State Park, with the Thomas Savage Visitor Center, www.dnr.state.mn.us/ state_parks/fort_snelling/index.html, and Fort Snelling Memorial Chapel.

23

A Search as Long as a River

Today the search is so easy.

Enter the enchantingly beautiful Itasca State Park in northern Minnesota and ask the ranger taking fees about the headwaters of the Mississippi River. Five miles straight ahead, she will patiently explain, as if the very same directions weren't posted on a sign just a few yards away.

And even those hints are hardly necessary, because most vehicles on the road that winds through the intense forest greenery are headed to the same parking lot and visitor center, near where a trail leads a short distance to a modest stream flowing out of sun-speckled Lake Itasca.

This was the place that had taunted and bedeviled the earliest searchers who came looking for the river's source, but that now delights thousands of modern-day explorers every year who come to tiptoe across the river on a string of slippery rocks, or to step across on a half-cut timber bridge, wondering for all the world how the mighty Mississippi, America's great wide waterway, the father of rivers, should come from such a trickle. They come from around the world, too. A Colorado man took my picture next to the historic headwaters' post, after we waited for a family in the traditional dress from India to have their own Kodak moment.

The post reads, as do the essential "I stepped across the Mississippi River" T-shirts and sweatshirts in the nearby gift shop, "Here 1,475 feet above the ocean the Mighty Mississippi begins, to flow on its winding way 2,552 miles away to the Gulf of Mexico."

"Here" was not easily discovered. The mouth of the Mississippi had been explored by Hernando de Soto as early as 1541, and Marquette and Joliet paddled stretches of the Upper Mississippi in 1673. But the actual source of the river was long a mystery that remained unsolved despite numerous efforts by explorers seeking not only the river's first drops of water, but also the fame certain to attend the men who found it.

Two years after Thomas Jefferson directed Lewis and Clark to explore the Missouri River in 1803 and to seek streams that would lead to the Pacific, army officer Zebulon Pike was authorized to lead a similar expedition to the headwaters of the Mississippi. Pike's party reached Leech Lake and raised an American flag at what he called the "main source of the Mississippi," but his trek fell short of the actual headwaters. In 1820 Lewis Cass, the territorial governor of Michigan, led another expedition to Upper Red Cedar Lake, where Pike had been fourteen years earlier, but the true source eluded that bunch as well.

Then came Giacomo Constantino Beltrami, a rather romantic explorer who longed for a place in history and thought discovering the source of the Mississippi River would provide it. After arriving in the United States in 1823, Beltrami made his way to northern Minnesota, where he eventually set out on his own. It was a hazardous journey before Beltrami, who had been abandoned by his Indian guides, made it to a heart-shaped lake that he named Julia, after a past romance, and declared that he had found the northern source of the Mississippi.

Seeking to cement his place in the explorers' pantheon, Beltrami later wrote two books about his expedition, linking his own name to those of Columbus, Marco Polo, and other intrepid discoverers, but his claims did nothing to convince most Americans the mystery had been solved. Nonetheless, his name was given to Beltrami County, which includes the headwaters region.

Credit for the discovery would go instead to Henry Rowe Schoolcraft, who had been part of the earlier Cass expedition. Schoolcraft was the Indian agent in the Lake Superior region, based in Sault Ste. Marie, and through the years—as well as through his marriage to Jane Johnston, the daughter of a fur trader and Indian woman—he became knowledgeable about the customs, legends, and language of the Chippewa, now known as the Ojibwe, people. Schoolcraft was also a dedicated author of books

Schoolcraft, ca. 1847. WHI IMAGE ID 23557

about Indian lore, but despite his considerable duties as agent, territorial legislator, and historical researcher, he was ever occupied with a desire to explore the headwaters of the Mississippi.

"Not only would such a discovery give him great prestige as an explorer," wrote historian Phillip Mason, "but it would serve as an excellent basis for another travel narrative."

Schoolcraft got his chance in 1832 when he was directed to proceed into Indian Territory to once again try to resolve hostilities between the historically warring Dakota and Chippewa, as well as to investigate the condition of the fur trade in the region. Others in the party included Dr. Douglass Houghton, who would later do much to develop northern Michigan and its rich resources; Lieutenant James Allen, who led a military escort; Reverend William Thurston Boutwell, who bore an eye toward evangelizing the Native people; and Schoolcraft's brother-in-law George Johnston, who, as half Indian, spoke several Indian dialects in addition to French and English and would serve as translator.

"If I do not see the 'veritable source' of the Mississippi, this time, it will not be from a want of the intention," Schoolcraft wrote to Cass before the group departed.

Schoolcraft's expedition differed in one significant way from those that had failed in the past: Schoolcraft was accompanied by an Indian guide, Ozawindib (various accounts use different spellings; Schoolcraft called him Oza Windib), who had agreed to lead the group to the headwaters. In his famous *Narrative of an Expedition through the Upper Mississippi to Lake Itasca*, published in 1834, Schoolcraft wrote that Ozawindib said, "My father, the country you are going to see is my hunting ground. I have traveled with you many days. I shall go with you farther. I myself will furnish the maps you have requested, and will guide you onward. There are many rapids in the way, but the waters are favorable. I shall consult with my band about the canoes, and see who will step forward to furnish them. My own canoe shall be one of them."

On July 13, the party reached their destination at Lac la Biche. Lt. Allen wrote in his journal that "there can be no doubt but that this is the true source and fountain of the longest and largest branch of the Mississippi." Schoolcraft similarly recorded the moment of discovery:

> We followed our guide down the sides of the last elevation, with the expectation of momentarily reaching the goal of our journey. What had been long sought, at last suddenly appeared. On turning out of a thicket, into a small weedy opening, the cheering sight of a transparent body of water burst upon our view. It was Itasca Lake—the source of the Mississippi.

Although Schoolcraft would later suggest the name came from a romantic Indian legend, historians agree Itasca was actually formed from the Latin words *veritas caput*, or true source. Schoolcraft took the –itas from *veritas* and ca- from *caput* to become Itasca.

Schoolcraft had traveled some 2,800 miles before he returned to Sault Ste. Marie, successful even beyond his historic discovery. The trip allowed more than two thousand Indians to be vaccinated against smallpox and, Mason wrote, "Few expeditions have surpassed the one of 1832 for the amount of information collected on the social life and customs of the American Indian."

But, Mason said, "It was the discovery of the true source of the Mississippi, rather than the storehouse of information on Indian conditions and the fur trade, which captured the popular imagination of the American public and gave Henry Rowe Schoolcraft his place among explorers."

Itasca State Park. WHI IMAGE ID 80443

Of course, not everyone accepted that place. Other explorers continued to travel to northern Minnesota, some hoping to discredit Schoolcraft and establish their own place in history. The most prominent of those was Willard Glazier, an ex-captain in the Civil War, who visited Lake Itasca in 1881 and, in less than one day of seeking, found an inlet on the west side of the lake that he declared the true source. He named it Lake Glazier, naturally, and went on to write several books supporting his claim, in some cases in language so close to Schoolcraft's own 1832 *Narrative* that Glazier was accused of plagiarism. Others attempted to debunk Glazier's claim, including the Minnesota Historical Society. Finally, in 1888, writer and surveyor Jacob V. Brower, who would later be called the "father of Lake Itasca," was able to discredit Glazier, legitimizing Schoolcraft's claim as the discoverer of the source of the Mississippi.

Brower's work brought such attention to Lake Itasca that, in 1891, Minnesota established Itasca Lake State Park. For all of its importance, however, the park had a troubled birth. Because no funding was approved, Brower, who was appointed the park's first superintendent, worked without pay and with little support. The second superintendent was paid, though not much, but was allowed to clear twenty acres of land to raise food for his family. Shortly after 1900, logging companies built a dam on the Mississippi River that backed up water into Lake Itasca and flooded nearby swamps. Despite opposition from supporters of the park, logging continued until the last large-scale operation was completed in 1919, threatening to change the natural landscape Schoolcraft had discovered.

Still, regal stands of virgin Norway and white pine were left behind, and after decades of care and nurturing the park has more trees than when it was established. And while Minnesota's oldest state park is immensely popular with visitors, and its beautiful forest greenery so cool and welcoming, it nonetheless remains a tranquil spot befitting its place as the home of the headwaters of the Mississippi, a park with some 150 lakes but no water more important than the trickle passing under a half-log footbridge that becomes the father of American rivers.

PLACES OF INTEREST

Itasca State Park, with more than thirty-two thousand forested acres and one hundred lakes, is about thirty miles southwest of Bemidji at Park Rapids, Minnesota. The Mary Gibbs Mississippi Headwaters Center and Jacob V. Brower Visitor Center feature interpretive displays and exhibits on park history, modern offerings, and more. www.dnr.state.mn.us/state_parks/itasca/index.html

Forest History Center, 2609 County Rd. 76, Grand Rapids, Minnesota, is a Minnesota Historical Society site focused on the state's forest history and logging days. www.dnr.state.mn.us/state_parks/itasca/index.html

24

Elsewhere on the River

On a recent trip back to Wisconsin from the Gulf Coast, our route crossed over some of America's major rivers: the Cumberland and the Tennessee, the Illinois and the Ohio. I savored a peek at each—but that's all you get at most river crossings, because modern bridges are designed to limit the staring off, lest that lead to *driving* off. One minute the river is there, the next it's in the rearview mirror.

That's why traveling upriver or down is always better than simply traveling across. Go with the flow, as they say, or against. It matters not.

In researching the stories for this book, I did indeed travel up and down the Mississippi River, but hardly for the first time. In the salad days of my newspaper life, back when I possessed a company Ford and an adequate expense account and was tasked with wandering near and far in search of stories, the Mississippi River was as much a go-to source of inspiration as any state park or historic place. Some offices come with lights and four walls, others with ribbons of highway and soaring river bluffs; long before I decided on a book called *This Storied River* the river had been giving me stories.

One summer I dedicated to driving the roads closest to the border of Wisconsin all the way around, from Milwaukee north to

The Cassville car ferry, ca. 1915. WHI IMAGE ID 95138

Marinette, west through Hurley to Superior and then south again, looking for material all the way. It occurred to me that much of the state's western border was river, not road, so in Alma I rented a houseboat and spent two delightful days puttering around on Lake Pepin, where the Mississippi runs wider than anywhere else. Mark Twain once said it was every boy's dream to be a riverboat captain, and for two days I was one. In the middle of the night, when I couldn't sleep, I sat on the deck and watched a tug pushing barges downriver, its ever vigilant spotlight sweeping from shore to shore, searching the darkness for trouble.

Did someone say Mark Twain? Another summer took me to Hannibal, Missouri, the boyhood home of Samuel Langhorne Clemens and the setting for Twain's iconic books. There are countless river towns on the Mississippi, but Hannibal wears the river better than most, and anyone who loved Tom Sawyer, which ought to be everyone, should see it.

One memory leads to another. On that same trip I visited historic Nauvoo, on a sublimely scenic bend in the Mississippi in Illinois. It was here that Joseph Smith and a band of Mormon followers settled in 1839 after being driven by conflict from Missouri. Distaste for the community's original name, Commerce, led Smith to change the name to Nauvoo, from a Hebrew word for "beautiful." The city today is still often called Beautiful Nauvoo, though the city's own story was not always so lovely. Conflicts, both among Mormon groups and with anti-Mormon forces, led to violence and death, including the murders of Smith and his brother, before most Mormons eventually left to travel west and resettle at Salt Lake City. Still, the Church of the Latter Day Saints still owns many historic buildings in Nauvoo today, operates a large visitor center here, and in 2002 dedicated a gleaming new temple.

A small cruiser at shore, near Cassville. WHI IMAGE ID 93632

Alma, as seen through Gerhard Gesell's camera. WHI IMAGE ID 25850

And the Quad Cities—Moline and Rock Island in Illinois, and Davenport and Bettendorf in Iowa—have many more than the few stories shared here. Chiropractic medicine was born in Davenport and is still taught there today. John Deere—the inventor, not a tractor—built his first plow factory in Moline in 1848, and the city still produces John Deere equipment there today, shipping much of it by rail on tracks that run along the river. Bettendorf was originally called Lillenthal, but the name was changed to honor the Bettendorf brothers who established a railroad car company that sold equipment nationwide.

The largest island in the Mississippi is there as well, a 946-acre tract that is home to the Rock Island Arsenal, a military

installation at which weapons have been produced for the US Army since 1862. Today's visitors can learn about that story through the Rock Island Arsenal Museum, with its huge collection of military weapons, and the Rock Island National Cemetery, covering more than seventy acres with more than twenty-four thousand grave markers.

Go north or south, on one side of the river or the other, and stories abound. If the Mississippi River is America's great waterway, the Great River Road is its greatest highway, passing through more than 110 counties and parishes in ten states. Technically it is not one road but many, all marked with the familiar green ship's wheel logo, and the sections that stretch through Wisconsin,

Iowa, Minnesota, and Illinois are deemed so especially beckoning they have been designated a National Scenic Byway.

For all the time I have spent on or along the river, I am hardly a river rat. As it happens I own a home on Lake Superior, as different a body of water from the Mississippi as red is from blue or Packers from Bears. But the river's stories are always present, the river's memories always pleasing, all rolling in the water of the little stream that flows from Lake Itasca and grows into the Mighty Mississippi, America's river.

Acknowledgments

As often has been said, there is no such thing as a free lunch. *This Storied River* came about when one day in late 2014 I shared a midday meal with the director of the Wisconsin Historical Society Press, Kathy Borkowski, who filled my belly with soup and my head with an idea for a book about the Mississippi River. The former was on the menu, the latter not something I had thought about until that day, but the prospect proved irresistible enough that before long I was on my way to Dubuque, where my research on these stories began.

It both amazes and delights me to say this is my third book for the Wisconsin Historical Society Press. Thanks to Kathy Borkowski and Kate Thompson for their willingness to work with me again, to developmental editor Carrie Kilman for so capably shepherding my manuscript through the production process, and to all those at the Press who helped with copy editing, photo selection, promotion, and all the other details that go into turning words into a book.

The history of the Mississippi and the vital role it has played in American life is collected in countless places up and down the great river from Lake Itasca to New Orleans. In compiling this collection of stories from the Upper Mississippi, I visited many museums and libraries, both for local history books and more recent newspaper accounts, and owe a debt of thanks to every such facility.

I will start, though, with the National Mississippi River Museum & Aquarium in Dubuque, Iowa, where the exceedingly helpful Tish Boyer, collections manager, graciously opened her archives for my inspection. More than that, Tish provided me with space to work, pulled file after file for my review, gave me a pencil when I lacked one for taking notes, and all in all made the first days of researching this book a pleasurable experience. The museum is highly recommended for anyone with an interest in the river.

Valuable material was also found in a number of other museums, including the Galena–Jo Daviess County Historical Society and U.S. Grant Museum in Galena, Illinois; the La Crosse Historical Society's Riverside Museum; the Lockmaster's House Heritage Museum in Guttenberg, Iowa; Winona County History Center and Polish Cultural Institute and Museum, both in Winona, Minnesota; Goodhue County Historical Society in Red Wing, Minnesota; Historic Fort Snelling in St. Paul, Minnesota; and the Mary Gibbs Mississippi Headwaters Center and Jacob V. Brower Visitor Center at the river's headwaters in Lake Itasca State Park. Thanks to all who work so hard to preserve and share the river's stories.

Thanks also to Robert Taunt of La Crosse for so willingly sharing his research on the tragic ending of the *War Eagle*.

Finally, though they couldn't have known they were helping at the time, I must acknowledge the contribution of all the editors at the *Milwaukee Journal* and *Milwaukee Journal Sentinel* who, over my twenty-five years as a newspaperman, allowed me to roam the river at will. Imagine that, a writer thanking editors. But I do.

Sources

"$5 Million Renaissance, Cruises to Boost Red Wing." *Rochester Post-Bulletin*, February 27, 2015.

Abraham Lincoln Online. "Lincoln in Galena, Illinois," www.abrahamlincoln online.org/lincoln/sites/galena.htm.

Ambrose, Stephen E., and Douglas Brinkley. *The Mississippi and the Making of a Nation*. National Geographic, 2003.

Anderson-Sannes, Barbara. *Alma on the Mississippi, 1848–1932*. Alma Historical Society, 1980.

Apps, Jerry. *Ringlingville USA: The Stupendous Story of Seven Siblings and Their Stunning Circus Success*. Wisconsin Historical Society Press, 2005.

Auge, Thomas. "The Life and Times of Julien Dubuque." *The Palimpsest*, State Historical Society of Iowa, January/February 1976.

Auto Touring Route: 1832 Black Hawk War. Published by War Trail Coalition, Mazomanie, WI.

Barry, John M. *Rising Tide: The Great Mississippi Flood of 1927 and How It Changed America*. Simon and Schuster, 1997.

Boser, Ulrich. "Galena, Illinois: Ulysses S. Grant's Postwar Retreat Is Not the Only Reason to Visit This Restored Victorian Showcase." Smithsonian.com, May 2007.

Botkin, B. A. *A Treasury of Mississippi River Folklore*. Bonanza Books, 1978.

Christenson, Jerome. "A Church Built from Hard Work by Winona's Polish Community." *Winona Daily News*, September 9, 2012.

Crutchfield, James A. *It Happened on the Mississippi River*. Globe Pequot Press, 2009.

Douglass, Michael. "The War of 1812 in Wisconsin." www.wisconsinhistory .org/turningpoints/search.asp?id=1620.

Drieslein, Rob. "The Mississippi Flood of 1965—Part 2." *Big River* Magazine, April 1994.

Dubuque Daily Herald, on the death of Diamond Jo Reynolds, February 25, 1891.

Dyrud, Martinus J. "History Talks from Prairie du Chien, Vol. 1." www .wisconsinhistory.org.turningpoints.

Eastman, Mary Henderson. *The Maiden's Rock, or, Wenona's Leap: Dahcotah, Or Life and Legends of the Sioux around Fort Snelling*, 1849.

Effigy Mounds. National Park Service booklet, Effigy Mounds National Monument, Iowa.

Fire Point Trail Guide. Merle W. Frommelt, park ranger. Effigy Mounds National Monument, Iowa.

Fremling, Calvin R. *Immortal River: The Upper Mississippi in Ancient and Modern Times.* University of Wisconsin Press, 2005.

Galena–Jo Daviess County Historical Society. "Galena History," www.galena history.org.

Galena Gazette, on the traffic jam at Grant's home, October 24, 1927.

Gauper, Beth. "Pike on the Prowl: For Better or Worse, America's First Emissary on the Upper Midwest Set History into Motion." www .midwestweekends.com, 2013.

Gibson, Michael D. "Julien Dubuque." *Biographical Dictionary of Iowa.* University of Iowa Press, 2015.

"The Good Father." *Waterski* Magazine, June 2006.

Guidebook to Stonefield Village. State Historical Society of Wisconsin, 1977.

Havighurst, Walter. *Upper Mississippi—a Wilderness Saga.* Rivers of America series. Farrar and Reinhart, 1944.

Hequet, Marc. "The Mississippi Flood of 1965—Part 1." *Big River* Magazine, March 1994.

Imrie, Robert. "Wisconsin to Apologize for 1832 Massacre of Sac and Fox Indians." Associated Press, May 2, 1990.

Jackson, Donald, ed. *Black Hawk: An Autobiography.* University of Illinois Press, 1955.

Jacobs, Walter W. *The First One Hundred Years: A History of Guttenberg, Iowa.* The Guttenberg Press, 1994.

Jalbert, Andrew J. "The Wreck of the Steamship War Eagle." *Big River* Magazine, July 2008.

Kashubian Capital of America. Compiled by Polish Cultural Institute and Museum, Winona, Minnesota.

Katz, Myer. *Echoes of Our Past: Vignettes of Historic La Crosse.* La Crosse Foundation, 1985.

Klinkenberg, Dean. Itasca State Park. www.mississippirivertraveler.com., 2012.

Klinkenberg, Dean. "Red Wing." *Minnesota Magazine,* Winter 2011.

Larson, Captain Ron. *Upper Mississippi River History—Fact, Fiction, Legend.* Steamboat Press, 1994.

Lass, William E. "Reynolds, Joseph 'Diamond Jo.'" *Biographical Dictionary of Iowa,* University of Iowa Press, 2009.

Mason, Philip P., ed. *The Search for the Great River's Source: An Account of Henry Rowe Schoolcraft's Expedition to the Source of the Mississippi River— Lake Itasca.* Prepared by the Minnesota State Park Interpretive Program, 1984.

Merrick, George B. "Joseph Reynolds and the Diamond Jo Line Steamers." *Proceedings of the Mississippi Valley Historical Association* 8, August 6, 1928.

Merrick, George Byron. *Old Times on the Upper Mississippi: The Recollections of a Steamboat Pilot from 1854 to 1863.* Fesler-Lampert Minnesota Heritage, 2001. Originally published by A. H. Clark and Company, 1909.

Middleton, Pat. *Discover! America's Great River Road.* Heritage Press, 2000.

Myers, Lena D. *Alexander MacGregor and His Town.* Published by McGregor (Iowa) Public Library, 1971.

Nissen, Ruth, and Wisconsin Department of Natural Resources. *Along the Mississippi River, Mussels, Clams Produce River Pearls.* Great River Publishing.

Petersen, William J. "Julien Dubuque." *The Palimpsest*, State Historical Society of Iowa, March 1966.

Petersen, William J. *Steamboating on the Upper Mississippi.* Dover, 1990.

Polish Settlers in Winona, Minnesota. Compiled by Polish Cultural Institute and Museum, Winona, Minnesota, 1958.

Rasmussen, C. A. *A History of the City of Red Wing, Minnesota.* Red Wing Advertising Company, 1933.

Richmond, Ben. "Clouds of Mayflies Are Terrorizing Wisconsin." Motherboard.vice.com, June 2014.

Rogers, Chris. "The Fight of Our Lives: How Winonans Battled the '65 Flood, and Won." *Winona Post*, April 19, 2015.

Sandlin, Lee. *Wicked River: The Mississippi When It Last Ran Wild.* Vintage Books, 2010.

Schneider, Paul. *Old Man River: The Mississippi River in North American History.* Henry Holt and Company, 2013.

Schoolcraft, Henry Rowe. *Narrative of an Expedition through the Upper Mississippi to Lake Itasca.* Published 1834.

Smith, Robert B. "Black Hawk War." *Military History*, February 1990.

"Steamer War Eagle Burned." *La Crosse Evening Democrat*, May 16, 1870.

"The Story of My Life" by Billie Button. Wisconsin Pearl Button Company, La Crosse, 1914.

Taunt, Robert B. *A Brief History of the Steamboat War Eagle.* La Crosse County Historical Society, May 2000.

Temte, Eric F. "The Pearl Button Industry Creates a Demand for Freshwater Mussels." University of Wisconsin–La Crosse graduate thesis, July 1968.

Trask, Kerry. *The Black Hawk War: The Battle for the Heart of America.* Henry Holt, 2006. Excerpted at www.wisconsinhistory.org.

Twain, Mark. *Life on the Mississippi.* 1883.

Visitor's Guide to Park History, Itasca State Park, Minnesota.

"Winona Gets First Hearing in New York." *Milwaukee Sunday Telegram,* April 22, 1923.

Young, Biloine Whiting. *River of Conflict, River of Dreams: Three Hundred Years on the Upper Mississippi.* Pogo Press, 2004.

Ziemer, Gregor. *A Daredevil and Two Boards: Ralph Samuelson, the Lake Pepin Pioneer Who Invented Water Skiing.* Hunter Halverson Press, 2006.

Index

Page numbers in **bold** refer to illustrations.

The Adventures of Huckleberry Finn (Twain), 7
African Americans: flood relief impact on, 134–135; slavery in the Northwest Territory, 156
"Akwa Skees," 131
Alim (Fox Indian chief), 62
Allen, James, 162
Alma, WI, **10**, 119–126; economic decline, 122–124; establishment of, 119–120; logging industry in, 120–123, **122–123**, **124**, 125; photos of, **120**, **125**, **170–171**; places of interest, 82, 126
Alma Area Museum, 126
Alma Historical Society, 120
Alma Journal and Beef Slough Advocate, 121
Alma on the Mississippi (Anderson-Sannes), 120, 121, 122–123
Ambrose, Stephen E., 6–7, 11, 95
American Eagle (steamboat), 105
American Indians: courting loyalty of, 57; lead mining, 20; river as home, 7; settlements in Winona area, 113–114
trade gatherings, 62–63. *See also* Ho-Chunk tribe; Meskwaki people; Sauk people; Seneca Indians; treaties and land cessions
American Queen (steamboat), 97, 105
American Ski Jumping Hall of Fame and Museum, 151
American Water Ski Association, 131
American Water Ski Hall of Fame, 131

Anderson-Sannes, Barbara, 120, 121, 122–123
Anson Northrup (steamboat), 4, **6**
Apps, Jerry, 46–47
aquaplanes, 128, **129**
Aquoqua (Kettle Chief), 14
Arizona, mining in, 53
Atkinson, Henry (General), 93
Auge, Thomas, 14–15

Bad Axe, Battle of, 89, **90**, 92–93, **93**, 95, 96
Bad Axe River, **10**, 89, 92
Baraboo, WI, 47
barges: for grain shipping, 50, 147; for railroad river crossings, 36; and river projects to aid traffic, 8, 37, 123
Barn Bluff, 151–152
Barry, John M., 134–135
Basilica of St. Stanislaus Kostka (Winona, MN), 116, 118
bateaus, and river exploration, 57–58
Battle of Bad Axe, 89, **90**, 92–93, **93**, 95, 96
Battle of Stillman's Run, 92
Bear Effigy Mound (Lake Koshkonong), **85**
Beaumont, William, 64–65, **65**, 68
Beckman, Charles, 149
Beef Slough Manufacturing, Booming, Long Driving and Transportation Company (BSMBLD&T), 121, 122
Beef Slough (WI) and logging industry, 121–123, **122–123**, 126
Beltrami, Giacomo Constantino, 160–161
Bena, MN, 38

Mines of Spain, **10**, 13–18
Mines of Spain Recreation Area, 13,
   15, 18
"Mingling of the Waters" ceremony,
   38
mining. *See* gold and silver mining;
   iron ore mining; lead mining;
   Mines of Spain
Minneapolis, MN, **10**, 58
Minnesota, on map, **10**
Minnesota Historical Society, 158,
   165, 166
Minnesota Marine Art Museum
   (Winona, MN), 118
Minnesota National Guard's First
   Regiment, 149
Minnesota River, 58, 135, 153, 155
missionaries, as settlers, 114, 146
*The Mississippi and the Making of a
   Nation* (Ambrose and Brinkley),
   6–7, 11, 95
Mississippi Logging Company, 121
Mississippi Queen (steamboat), 4
Mississippi River, **8–9**; about, 6–12;
   at confluence with Minnesota
   River, 58, 135, 153; at confluence
   with Wisconsin River, 55, 57, 62,
   68; discovery of clam beds, 71;
   engineering projects, 8–9, 35–38,
   39, 123; river communities,
   167–172. *See also* floods and high
   water; headwaters of the Missis-
   sippi; Upper Mississippi River
Mississippi River Pearl Jewelry
   Company (Alma, WI), 81, 82
Missouri River, 57, 160
Moline, IL, 170
Monroe, WI, 18
Montezuma (now Winona), MN,
   113, 115. *See also* Winona, MN
Mormon groups, 169
Morton, Mary, 50
mounds. *See* Effigy Mounds
   National Monument

Muscatine, IA: button and pearl
   industries, 71, 75, **78**; places of
   interest, 76, 82
Muscatine Journal, 52
musical entertainment on steamboats, 5, 104
mussels, freshwater. *See* clams and
   clammers; pearl button manufacturing; pearls and pearl
   prospecting

*Narrative of an Expedition through the
   Upper Mississippi to Lake Itasca*
   (Schoolcraft), 162–163, 165
Natchez (steamboat), 104
National Guard, and floods, 136
National Historic Landmarks and
   Districts, 68, 124, 158
National Mississippi River Museum
   & Aquarium (Dubuque): 7, 70;
   and personal Grand Excursion,
   12; visitor information, 18, 54,
   60, 82, 106
national park proposals, 84–85
National Park Service, on river wild-
   life, 11
National Register of Historic Places,
   19, 38, 44
National Rivers Hall of Fame, 54, 60
National Scenic Byway designation,
   11, 171–172. *See also* Great River
   Road
Native Americans. *See* American
   Indians
natural pearls. *See* pearls and pearl
   prospecting
Nauvoo, IL, 169
Nelson Dewey State Park (WI), 29,
   30
New Haven Register, 2
New Orleans, LA, 38
New York Tribune, 2
Newberry family, 29
North McGregor, IA, 43

About the Author

Dennis McCann spent most of his professional life traveling across Wisconsin and the Midwest for the *Milwaukee Journal* and *Milwaukee Journal Sentinel*. A Wisconsin native and graduate of the University of Wisconsin-Madison, McCann is the author of several books of Wisconsin travel and history, including *This Superior Place: Stories of Bayfield and the Apostle Islands* and *Badger Boneyards: The Eternal Rest of the Story*, both published by the Wisconsin Historical Society Press. He and his wife, Barbara, a retired teacher, reside in Bayfield.

PHOTO BY BARBARA MCCANN